This book should be returned to any branch of the
Lancashire County Library on or before the date

Lancashire County Library
Bowran Street
Preston PR1 2UX

Lancashire
County Council

www.lancashire.gov.uk/libraries

HOOKED

ON

CROCHET

Ruth Maddock

HOOKED

ON

CROCHET

BLOOMSBURY

LONDON · NEW DELHI · NEW YORK · SYDNEY

Bloomsbury Visual Arts
An imprint of Bloomsbury Publishing Plc

50 Bedford Square   1385 Broadway
London   New York
WC1B 3DP   NY 10018
UK   USA

www.bloomsbury.com

Bloomsbury is a registered trade mark of
Bloomsbury Publishing Plc

© Ruth Maddock, 2014

British Library
Cataloguing-in-Publication Data
A catalogue record for this book is available
from the British Library.

ISBN: Flexi: 978-1-4081-9192-7

Library of Congress
Cataloging-in-Publication Data
Maddock, Ruth.
Hooked on crochet / Ruth Maddock.
pages cm
Includes index.

ISBN 978-1-4081-9192-7 (paperback)
1. Crocheting. I. Title.
TT820.M237 2014
746.43'4--dc23
2014015045

Cover design by Evelin Kasikov
Text design by Evelin Kasikov
Typeset by Precision Graphics
Printed and bound in China

Contents

Introduction

Creativity is a fact of life; we are all born with it, and all yearn to express it in our own unique and individual way. How we express it displays the very core of our being to others. Crochet is one of the many ways to express this creativity and one that many people aspire to. People of all ages and from all walks of life come to my crochet classes and there is a renewed interest in this lovely craft. Leading designers such as Dolce and Gabbana, Paul Smith and Prada have recently featured crochet on their catwalks and it has been worn by celebrities such as Sarah Jessica Parker, Mariah Carey and Jennifer Aniston.

Crochet has many advantages. Not only is it an outlet for your creativity, it also has the beneficial side effect of helping you to de-stress and relax. It is portable, uses minimal tools and can be done 'on the go' or while waiting for buses, planes or appointments. And it's also great for evenings in watching the telly!

This book will take you on a journey into the world of crochet. As a complete beginner you will learn the very basic steps and by building on these you will acquire all the skills needed to follow patterns and make your own projects. You will soon know the joy of being able to say 'I made this myself'.

Those of you who can already do the crochet basics will find this book an invaluable resource to dip in and out of and to brush up on your skills and correct any problems.

I love to crochet, and in particular I love the diversity of fabrics, textures and designs that can be created using yarns from the very fine to the super thick. As I have been writing crochet patterns and teaching crochet for many years, I understand the difficulties that you may face as you begin to create using just a hook, some yarn and a pattern that appears to be written in a foreign language. Drawing on this experience I will provide insightful tips and tricks along the way as you start to master this craft.

Small simple projects accompany each step of the learning process and I hope that these will inspire you and give you tremendous enjoyment and satisfaction as you move from stage to stage.

Happy crocheting!

Ruth Maddock

Crocheting while enjoying a coffee.

1 Basics

ESSENTIAL TOOLS

One of the really good things about crochet is that it requires very little in the way of equipment.

Apart from basic sewing equipment such as scissors, a tape measure, pins and large-eyed sewing or tapestry needles, the only essential equipment that you need is a crochet hook and some yarn. This all makes it very portable.

Crochet hooks come in a variety of shapes and sizes. The size of hook that you will use is governed by the thickness of the yarn. There are many different styles of hook, but to begin I suggest that you use a basic metal hook like those shown here.

Those of us who knit and crochet also have a secret obsession. When it comes to yarn shops we are drawn like moths to a flame. Holidays cause particular excitement as they provide the opportunity for foraging in new locations. Once there, credit cards are not safe and we invariably leave with bags of yummy new yarns to add to our stash. This compulsion is not helped by the yarn companies and independent dyers, who keep producing the most amazing new yarns in ever-increasing varieties of colour, weight, fibre and texture. As you progress with your crochet skills you will develop favourite yarns that you are repeatedly drawn back to.

However, for the purposes of beginning to learn to crochet – and at the risk of being terribly boring – I suggest that you use a basic double knit (DK) thickness yarn in a light – or bright – colour.

Basic crochet hooks
in the various sizes.

Basic balls of yarn.

NON-ESSENTIAL TOOLS

Posh crochet hooks

As I have already said, crochet hooks come not only in different sizes but also in a variety of shapes. They can be made from many different materials such as aluminium, plastic, bone, bamboo and various types of hardwood such as birch. Crochet hooks can also be made from steel, but these usually have a different numbering system and are used for very fine work. Once you have some crocheting experience you may want to experiment with other shapes and styles of hook to see if they suit you better. Some can be quite expensive so it's a good idea to try them out before you invest in them. If you have a problem with mobility in your hands and wrists the type of hook that you use can make a big difference to your comfort when crocheting.

A selection of beautiful hand-finished crochet hooks made in birch from Brittany Needles and Hooks.

Some different ways of marking stitches.

Stitch markers

Different from those used for knitting, the markers used
for crochet are attached to the stitch rather than the
needle. These markers are sometimes referred to as
split-ring stitch markers or open stitch markers, as they
have an open slot that can be hung on individual stitches.
However, instead of buying specialist markers you could
use small safety pins, paperclips or pieces of contrasting
coloured thread.

Wool sewing needle

Used for sewing seams in your work, wool sewing
needles can be bought from yarn shops. They are usually
blunted and have a large eye so that they can be threaded
with thick yarns. Any sewing needle with an eye large
enough for the yarn to be threaded through will do
the job.

Yarn holder

Yarn holders can be beautiful hand-crafted pots, or
simple jars or boxes with a hole in the lid. They are used
for holding balls of yarn to prevent them from rolling all
over the floor.

This beautiful yarn pot is made by Caractacus
Pots. Caractacus Pots makes a range of unique
yarn bowls sold through the Folksy shop
http://folksy.com/shops/CaractacusPots.

ABOUT HOOKS

All hooks have a blunt rounded end (the point or tip) that can easily be pushed into the stitch or space, a 'throat' which is the bit that actually does the 'hooking', a shank, which is where the stitch sits (this determines the size of the stitch), and a handle. Most, but not all, also have a thumb rest.

The point or tip   The thumb rest

The throat   The shank   The handle

The parts of a crochet hook.

Hook sizes

Apart from the shape and design of the hook, there are many different sizes of hook, and these are measured in metric units. However if you have inherited a set from an elderly relative or bought some in a charity shop, they may well be in the old UK sizes. The numbering of hooks in the US is different and you need to be aware of this as some books available in the UK – often those found in the discount bookshops – have originated in the US. The American numbering system uses a letter followed by a number. This number is the equivalent US knitting needle size.

ABOUT YARNS

There is an incredible array of yarns on the market. Visit your local yarn shop and your senses will be both amazed and delighted. Never before have there been so many gorgeous yarns to choose from. But beware: whilst the frilly, fluffy, lumpy and embellished yarns are great for knitting, you will usually need to steer clear of them if you are going to crochet.

Crochet is a way of making a fabric that creates a texture or lace pattern that needs to be visible. If you try to crochet using these novelty yarns, much of the pattern will be lost. These yarns can also be very difficult to crochet with; in particular they can often be almost impossible to unravel – which is something you may do quite a bit as you learn to crochet.

Metric Size	UK Size	US Size
2.00 mm	14	-
2.25 mm	13	B/1
2.50 mm	12	-
2.75 mm	-	C/2
3.00 mm	11	-
3.25 mm	10	D/3
3.50 mm	9	E/4
3.75 mm	-	F/5
4.00 mm	8	G/6
4.50 mm	7	7
5.00 mm	6	H/8
5.50 mm	5	I/9
6.00 mm	4	J/10
6.50 mm	3	K/10½
7.00 mm	2	-
8.00 mm	0	L/11
9.00 mm	00	M/13
10.00 mm	000	N/15

Hook size conversion chart.

Yarn fibres

Traditional yarns were made from fibres such as wool, cotton, linen, cashmere, alpaca and silk. But with modern technology we now have yarns made from stinging nettles, milk, bamboo, bananas and many kinds of recycled products, such as recycled Indian saris. In addition to these, technology is able to create novelty synthetics that look and feel like fur or suede or have attached sequins, beads, textures and bobbles.

Yarns can also be dyed in many different ways so that they create complex colour patterns when crocheted or knitted. Many independent yarn dyers advertise their products on sites such as eBay (www.ebay.co.uk), Etsy (www.etsy.com), and Folksy (www.folksy.co.uk); these yarns are known collectively as indie yarns. Some of them are truly scrumptious.

A selection of different yarns.

Hand-dyed 100% merino wool, this quality is DK weight 'Desire' shade Rhubarb Crumble by The Skein Queen. Similar yarns are available at www.skeinqueen.co.uk.

Yarn thickness

Although yarns can be made from many different fibres and have amazing textures and colours, they are usually classified by thickness. In the UK we use terms such as 4 ply, DK, Aran and chunky to describe the thickness of yarn. However, thickness is not standardised across the industry and can vary. The same is true of yarns in other countries, where different names are used to refer to different thicknesses of yarn.

The important information regarding thickness can be found on the ball-band or label. Ball-bands give information about the fibres used, the washing instructions, the yarn spinner and the country of manufacture. They also give the tension or gauge – the only true way of knowing if the yarn you want to buy is right for your pattern. Tension is the word used to describe how many stitches there are in 10 cm (4 in) of work. This is important when choosing yarns and especially when substituting one yarn for another. On ball-bands tension is usually given as a knitting measurement.

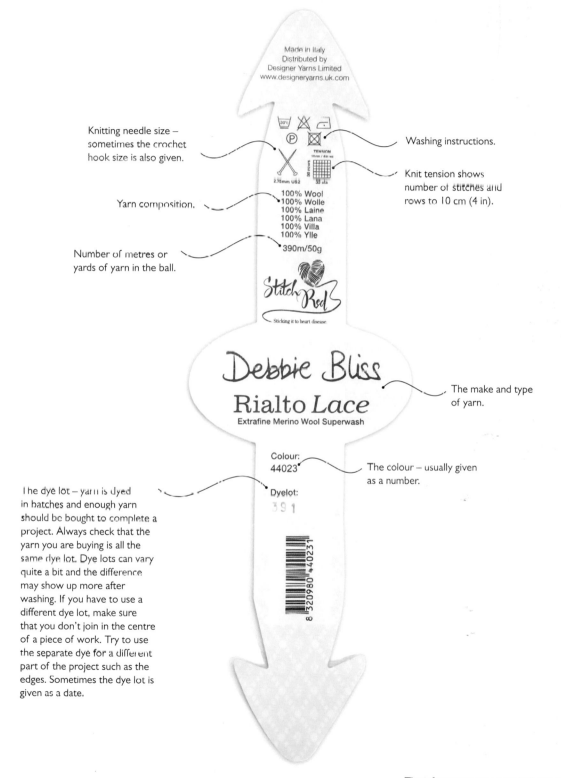

Knitting needle size –
sometimes the crochet
hook size is also given.

Washing instructions.

Knit tension shows
number of stitches and
rows to 10 cm (4 in).

2.75mm US2

TENSION
10cm / 4in sq

50 rows

33 sts

Yarn composition.

100% Wool
100% Wolle
100% Laine
100% Lana
100% Villa
100% Ylle

Number of metres or
yards of yarn in the ball.

390m/50g

Stitch Red
Sticking it to heart disease

Made in Italy
Distributed by
Designer Yarns Limited
www.designeryarns.uk.com

Debbie Bliss

Rialto Lace
Extrafine Merino Wool Superwash

The make and type
of yarn.

Colour:
44023

The colour – usually given
as a number.

Dyelot:
391

The dye lot – yarn is dyed
in batches and enough yarn
should be bought to complete a
project. Always check that the
yarn you are buying is all the
same dye lot. Dye lots can vary
quite a bit and the difference
may show up more after
washing. If you have to use a
different dye lot, make sure
that you don't join in the centre
of a piece of work. Try to use
the separate dye for a different
part of the project such as the
edges. Sometimes the dye lot is
given as a date.

The information on a yarn ball-band.

Once upon a time, the word 'ply' meant a single strand of yarn. These single strands of yarn can be any thickness, such as the Lopi yarns created from the fleece of the Icelandic sheep which, although being a loosely-spun single ply, have a chunky thickness. When several plies of yarn were twisted together this would create yarn that was labelled 2 ply, 3 ply, 4 ply and so on. Because the yarn used was nearly always wool spun to a similar thickness, the thickness of the yarns produced was pretty standard and so the various 'plies' of yarn began to mean a thickness of yarn rather than a number of yarn strands twisted together.

If you are going to spend your time crocheting beautiful creations – especially garments – you will need to know that the yarn you buy will create a project that ends up the intended size. If you buy the yarn stated in the pattern, this should be no problem – although you will still have to check that your work measures the same as that given in the pattern.

However, if you want to use a different yarn you will only be able to match the tension given in the pattern if your chosen yarn is the same thickness as the one specified. The only true way to do this is to match the knitting tension, which will be given on the ball-band. If the yarn in the pattern has been discontinued this can create difficulties, but an internet search can usually help.

Thin ← ⟶ **Thick**

Common names	Cobweb 1 ply	Lace 2 ply	Light Fingering 3 ply	Fingering Sock Yarn 4 ply	Sport Quicker knit 5 ply	Light Worsted Double Knit (DK) 8 ply	Worsted Afghan Aran 10 ply	Bulky Chunky Craft 12 ply	Super Bulky Super Chunky Craft 12 ply
WPI*	30–36	24	18–20	14	12	11	8–9	7	5–6
Knitted tension or gauge worked in stocking stitch & measured over 10 cm (4 in)	40–44 sts	36–38 sts	32–34 sts	28–30 sts	24–26 sts	22–24 sts	18–20 sts	14–16 sts	8–12 sts
Knitting needle size	2 mm UK 14 US 1	2.75 mm UK 12 US 2	3 mm UK 11 US 2–3	3.25 mm UK 10 US 3–4	3.75 mm UK 9 US 5	4 mm UK 8 US 6	4.5 mm UK 7 US 7	5 mm UK 6 US 8	8–10 mm UK 00–000 US 11–15
Crochet tension or gauge worked over double crochet & measured over 10 cm (4 in)			32–42	21–32	16–20	12–17	11–14	8–11	5–9
Crochet hook size	2–2.5 mm UK 14–12 US B/1	2–2.5 mm UK 14–12 US B/1	2.25 mm UK 13 US B/1	3–3.5 mm UK 13 US B/1	3.5–4 mm UK 9–8 US E/4–G/6	4–5.5 mm UK 8–5 US G/6–I/9	5.5–6.5 mm UK 5–3 US I/9–K/10.5	6.5–8 mm UK 3–0 US K/10.5–L/11	8 mm and larger UK 0 US L/11

Yarn thickness, common names and tensions.

Measuring wraps per inch.

*Wraps per inch (WPI)

Wraps per inch is an alternative way of working out how thick a yarn is. More often used in the US, it is handy if your yarn has no ball-band. WPI is a measurement that states how many threads there are to an inch (2.5 cm).

To measure wraps per inch it is best to use a round object such as a broom handle or a pencil. Cut a length of yarn from the ball and wrap this – without stretching it – around your broomstick so that each wrap of yarn sits next to its neighbour without overlapping. You need to wrap for a good 5 cm (2 in), then fix the ends with some sticky tape. Use a ruler to measure how many wraps there are in one inch (2.5 cm).

Cotton yarns and steel hooks

For very fine crochet work, cotton yarns come in a range of thicknesses up to the approximate knitting yarn weight of 4 ply. These cotton yarns usually come on spools and have a numbering system that increases with the thinness of the yarn, so that a number 40 yarn is much thinner than a number 10. These yarns are crocheted using very fine steel hooks.

PATTERNS AND ABBREVIATIONS

Generally, in order to make a project you will need to follow a pattern. A pattern is a list of instructions – like a recipe – that will ensure that your project turns out like the one in the picture. All crochet patterns are worked using only a few basic stitches: chain stitch, slip stitch, double crochet stitch and various lengths of treble stitches.

When you first look at a pattern you may think it is written in a foreign language and impossible to follow, but as you work through line by line you will discover that it really isn't that difficult.

For simplicity, patterns are written using a range of abbreviations, such as 'ch' (chain), 'tr' (treble) and 'st' (stitch). As with yarn thicknesses, abbreviations are not standardised, so you may come across a number of different ways of stating the same thing, however all patterns should give you this information.

Patterns also make use of asterisks: *. These are used to mark the beginning of a sequence of stitches, or a section of pattern that is to be repeated. When there are a number of asterisks together, they indicate that there are a number of different sections of work that are to be repeated.

Brackets, which can be square [ ] or round ( ), are used when there are different instructions for different sizes. For instance, a pattern might say: make a length of 3(6:8:11) chain, and in this case the different figures refer to the number of chain required for the different sizes. When following a pattern with a number of different sizes you will use the numbers given at the same place within the brackets throughout the work. If the figure for your size is '0' then that instruction should be omitted.

Brackets are also used to show a pattern sequence that is to be repeated a given number of times. For instance: (3 ch, 1 tr in next stitch) x 3, means that the sequence inside the brackets is repeated three times.

A commercial crochet pattern.

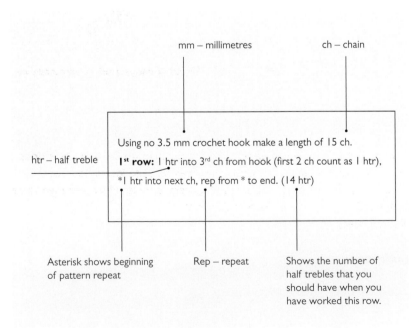

mm – millimetres   ch – chain

Using no 3.5 mm crochet hook make a length of 15 ch.

1st row: 1 htr into 3rd ch from hook (first 2 ch count as 1 htr), *1 htr into next ch, rep from * to end. (14 htr)

htr – half treble

Asterisk shows beginning of pattern repeat

Rep – repeat

Shows the number of half trebles that you should have when you have worked this row.

Example of a pattern, showing the abbreviations used.

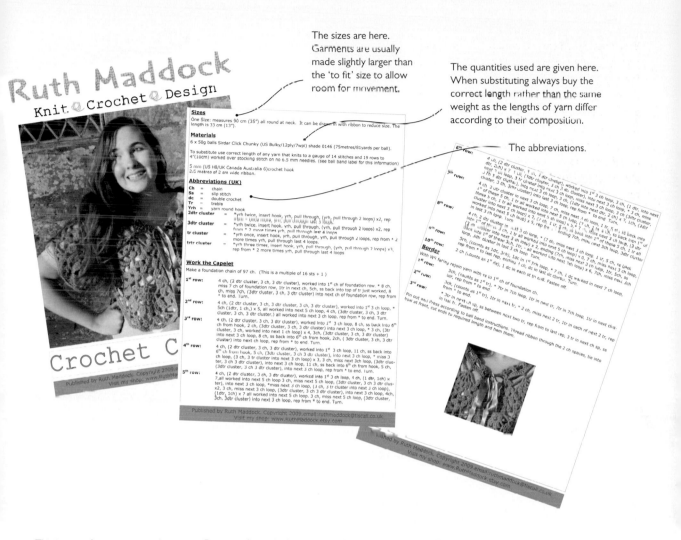

The sizes are here. Garments are usually made slightly larger than the 'to fit' size to allow room for movement.

The quantities used are given here. When substituting always buy the correct length rather than the same weight as the lengths of yarn differ according to their composition.

The abbreviations.

This is one of my commercial patterns. Patterns always look more complicated than they are. Don't be afraid to get stuck in. Your local yarn shop or the pattern publisher should be able to help if you don't understand the pattern.

The style of a pattern, the way it is written and the abbreviations used all differ depending on who wrote or published the pattern. They also differ from country to country. However, each pattern will have basic information about size, the yarn and hooks you need, the tension of your work and the abbreviations. The abbreviations for all the patterns in this book can be found on page 126.

Some patterns use charts to show how to work various stitch patterns. These can be quite intimidating, but become clear as you begin to work. However, I won't be using charts in this book.

TENSION

As we have seen, in order for your finished product to be the size stated in the pattern you will need to match your tension to that of the pattern writer. Most crochet patterns will state this tension and you will need to do a small test piece of work in order to check this. The tension instructions for the fingerless gloves on page 56 states:

'In order for the gloves to be the size given you will need to work to a tension of 16 trebles and 9 rows to 10 cm (4 in) square.'

It will usually be left to you to work out how to make this small piece of work to measure. Whilst you should always check your tension, it is sometimes easiest to start working your first pattern piece and then measure the number of stitches and rows after working a few rows. But if the sizing is critical, you must be prepared to rip out and start again – using a smaller hook if your work is too large or a larger hook if your work is too small.

When measuring the work you should always use a flat surface. Trying to measure it on your lap in front of the telly really doesn't work. If you have to make a choice it is usually better to make the number of stitches (the width) correct, as the number of rows (the length) can often be altered while working.

TIP

For your first project in crochet, choose something that doesn't need to be a particular size so that the tension is not important.

Measure your tension in the middle of a piece of work to give more accurate results.

HOLDING THE HOOK

I spent a good twenty years of my crocheting history holding the hook and yarn as if I was knitting. This produced very good results and I didn't really need to change. However, when I decided to try holding the hook and yarn 'correctly' I found crocheting much easier – although it took a while to master. My experience demonstrates that you really can hold the hook any way you like, especially when you are starting out. If you get really hung up about holding the hook 'correctly' you may achieve very little. It's far better to make some progress by producing some uneven chain bracelets, interesting owls and wonky drinks mats. Later, when you have a bit of experience, you can start 'worrying' about correct techniques – if you want to.

These are the two main ways to hold the hook:

TIP

Holding the hook and yarn correctly is easier once you have worked a few rows.

This method is usually referred to as holding the hook like a knife.

This method is usually referred to as holding the hook like a pencil. This is the way I hold the hook.

The 'correct' way to hold the yarn:

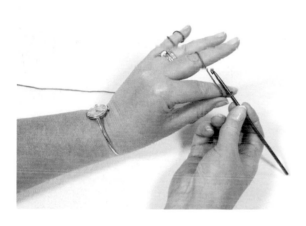

The yarn is wound around the fingers of the left hand to create tension for the working part of the yarn, which is the straight length of yarn between the index and middle fingers. The work on the hook is held between the thumb and the index finger of the left hand. You can wind the yarn around your fingers in any way that seems comfortable, just as long as this creates some tension in the yarn.

Left-handed crocheters

I have taught a number of left-handers to crochet. Many are partially ambidextrous and after trying both hands will settle on working in a right-handed way. However, for those of you who need to hold the yarn in the right hand and the hook in the left, the instructions in this book can be reversed, either by looking at the book in a mirror or by photocopying the instruction photos using the mirror-image setting. There are also a number of useful instructional videos on YouTube. Once you have mastered the art of the basic crochet stitches you will discover that most crochet patterns are written by and for right-handed people. However, if you are a left-handed crocheter you will:

- Work the stitches from the left-hand side of the row towards the right-hand side (right-handers work from right to left).

- Work rounds of crochet clockwise (right-handers work in an anti-clockwise direction).

- Note that any diagonal stitch patterns will create diagonals that run in the opposite direction.

- Need to adapt patterns reversing any instructions given such as 'right-hand side', 'work the chart from right to left', or 'join at right-hand corner'.

The chain stitch and the slip stitch

Now that you have some idea about hooks, yarns and pattern instructions, you can begin to make some crochet stitches. All crochet begins with at least one chain stitch, and these chain stitches begin with a slip knot.

To make a slip knot

The slip knot is the first loop or chain on the hook. There are a number of ways to make a slip knot, but here is one of the easiest.

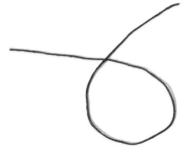

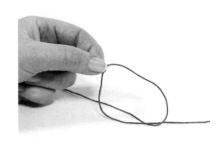

STEP 1 Lay the end of the yarn on a flat surface and wind round to form a circle with the yarn from the ball under the tail end of the yarn.

STEP 2 Pick up this circle and place it on top of the yarn end that comes from the ball.

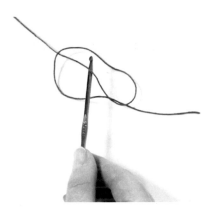

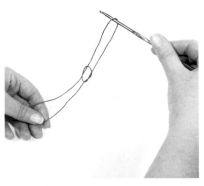

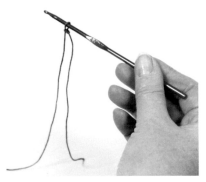

STEP 3 Insert your hook under the yarn that now forms the straight line in the middle.

STEP 4 Lift your hook and you will see that a large loop has been formed.

STEP 5 Pull the tail end to tighten the loop so that it fits the hook snugly but not too tightly.

To make a chain stitch (ch)

Now that you have a loop on the hook, you can begin to make some chains. Don't worry about how you are holding the hook at this stage, but begin to work as follows:

STEP 1 Place the yarn (from the ball end) over the hook from the back of the hook to the front (the yarn goes over the hook in an anti-clockwise direction). This is called 'yarn over hook' (yoh). If you are holding the hook as shown in the photo you will create this 'yarn over hook' by moving the hook under the yarn held between the index and forefinger of the left hand.

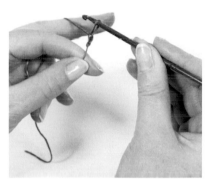

TIP

Don't worry if your stitches are loose and holey, but if they are very tight, try to loosen them a little.

STEP 2 Holding the work near the knot of the slip stitch and, with the throat of the hook facing towards you – or slightly downwards, pull on the end of the hook until the yarn over the hook comes through the loop on the hook. This is your first chain stitch. Make this chain stitch nice and loose.

STEP 3 Repeat steps 1 and 2 to make more chain stitches in the same way. Continue until you have enough chain stitches to fit around your wrist.

Chain stitches are used as the first row of most projects and are often referred to as the foundation row.

When you have made a few chain stitches you will notice that each stitch has three strands and there appears to be a front and a back to the stitches. It is important that you can identify each separate stitch so that you can count the number of chain stitches that you have worked.

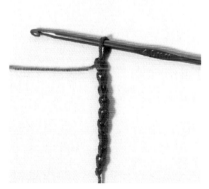

The front of the chain stitch is smooth and looks like a 'v' shape.

The back of the chain stitch is bumpy. These bumps run vertically and are behind the 'v' shapes on the front.

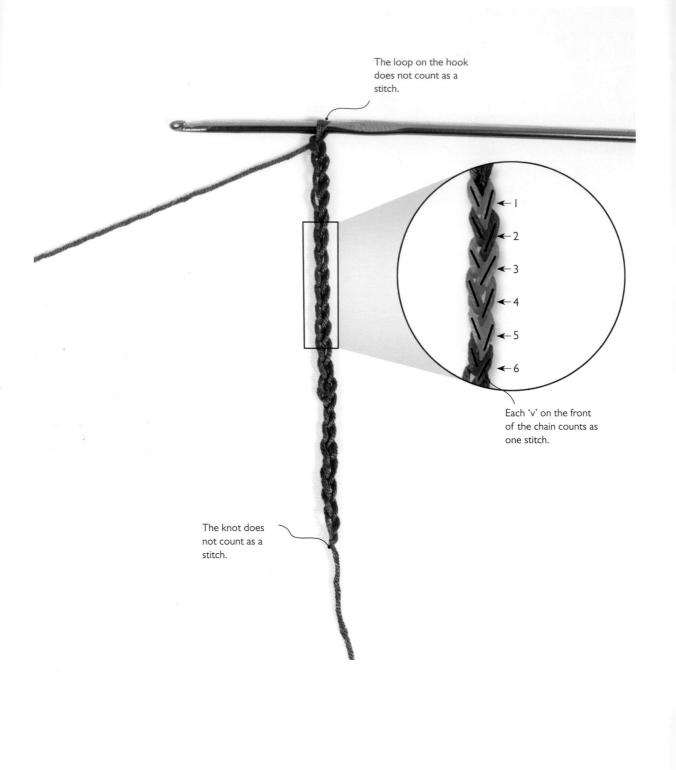

The loop on the hook does not count as a stitch.

Each 'v' on the front of the chain counts as one stitch.

← 1
← 2
← 3
← 4
← 5
← 6

The knot does not count as a stitch.

To make a slip stitch (ss)

You can join these chain stitches into a circle by using a slip stitch. The slip stitch is used to join work when forming a circle or ring, or during the course of a stitch pattern. It can be used to make a length of cord and is also used when shaping crochet.

STEP 1 Take the length of chain that you have already made and, keeping the last loop on the hook, insert the hook into the first chain that you made. You now have two loops on the hook.

STEP 2 Place the yarn over the hook as if you were making another chain.

STEP 3 Pull on the end of the hook so that the yarn over the hook passes through both the loops on the hook. You will now have only one loop on the hook and your length of chain will have formed a circle.

How to fasten off

Make the loop on the hook slightly bigger and then remove it from the hook. Cut the end of the yarn and bring it through this loop. Pull tightly to finish. You can knot the ends together firmly then cut them off, or weave in the ends – see instructions on page 25.

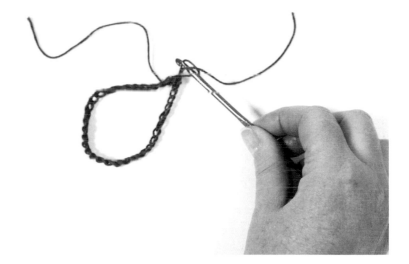

CROCHET WRISTBAND

Worked using only crochet chain, this super simple wristband is the perfect beginner's project.

Size
These wristbands can be made to fit any size wrist.

Materials
- oddments of any DK yarn (I used Rico Design Essentials Cotton DK, 50 g balls in a selection of shades (130 m/143 yd per ball))

- 1 x 4 mm crochet hook (USE/4)

- wool sewing needle

Tension
Tension is not important for this project.

Rico Design Essentials Cotton DK.

Wristband

Using a 4 mm hook, make a length of chain using the instructions given above. When the length of chain fits loosely round your wrist, join the first and last chains with a slip stitch. Fasten off and weave in the ends.

You can work these wristbands in all sorts of colours and thicknesses of yarn. As you get more experienced you may want to add beads and charms.

This simple wristband is your first completed project.

How to weave in ends

Thread the yarn end on to a needle and sew or weave through the stitches so that the end is hidden and secure, then cut the yarn end off. On a small project like this flower or the wristband, it is slightly more tricky than on a larger project where there is more 'fabric' to weave through.

Wear several wristbands together.

CROCHET FLOWER

By adding slip stitch to your skills you can now make this pretty flower. The stitches used for this pattern are chain (ch) and slip stitch (ss).

Size
The flower can be any size: the ones shown in the photo measure approximately 5 cm (2 in) across.

Materials
- oddments of any DK yarn (I used Rico Design Essentials Cotton DK, 50 g balls in a selection of shades (130 m/143 yd per ball))

- 1 x 4 mm crochet hook (USE/4)

- 1 large and 1 small button

- brooch back or keyring chain – from your local craft store or eBay

- wool sewing needle

Tension
Tension is not important for this project.

Abbreviations
ch = chain
ss = slip stitch
rep = repeat
yoh = yarn over hook

How to work into a crochet ring

The flower uses slip stitches worked into the ring as follows: insert hook into the ring (not into a stitch), yoh, draw back through the ring *and* through the loop on the hook.

Small flower

Using a 4 mm hook, make a length of 4 ch, join to the first ch with a ss to form a ring. Now work * 6 ch, then 1 ss worked into the ring, rep from * 6 times in all. Fasten off, cut the yarn and weave in the ends.

Remember: An asterisk in the pattern indicates where a pattern sequence begins.

Large flower

Using a 4 mm hook and a different colour, make a length of 4 ch, join to the first ch with a ss to form a ring. Now work * 10 ch, then 1 ss into the ring, rep from * 10 times in all. Fasten off and cut the yarn, leaving a long end (about 30 cm/12 in) for making up.

Making up

Place the small flower in the centre of the large flower and use the long end of yarn from the large flower to sew the two together. Sew one or two buttons into the centre. If required, using the yarn still threaded onto the needle, sew a brooch back or keyring chain to the back of the flower. Weave in any remaining ends.

Now that you have made the flower you will be able to make a floral wristband.

This is the finished flower, which can be used in a variety of ways.

With an added key chain the flower makes a great key fob.

The finished flower also makes a pretty brooch.

FLORAL WRISTBAND

Combine the wristband with the flower and you have the perfect summer's day accessory.

Size
The wristband can be made to fit any size wrist.

Materials
- oddments of any DK yarn (I used Rico Design Essentials Cotton DK, 50 g balls in a selection of shades (130 m/143 yd per ball))

- 1 x 4 mm crochet hook (USE/4)

- wool sewing needle

Tension
Tension is not important for this project.

Abbreviations
ch = chain
ss = slip stitch

The floral wristband makes a pretty summer accessory.

Make the wristband

Using a 4 mm hook, make a length of chain. When the length of chain fits loosely round your wrist seven times, join to the first ch with ss and fasten off, leaving a long end (about 30 cm/12 in) for making up.

Making up

Arrange the length of chain into seven loops and join together by winding the long end of yarn around all seven loops. Sew in the end firmly and then use this end to sew on a flower (see instructions for the flower on pages 26–27).

Although the slip stitch is more commonly used to join circles or as part of a stitch pattern, it can be used on its own. Working a row of slip stitches into a foundation row of chain creates a thick cord, which is useful when creating ties and cords for garments and jewellery.

To make a row of slip stitches

STEP 1 Create a length of 15 chain. This will be your foundation row.

STEP 2 Insert the hook under one strand of the second chain from the hook. Do not count the loop on the hook.

TIP

You can choose whether to insert your hook either under one or two strands of each chain in the foundation row. However, you should always be consistent. Generally, when working under one strand you achieve a looser edge than when working under two strands.

STEP 3 Bring the yarn over the hook and draw it through both loops on the hook. Working the slip stitch can feel a little awkward, but don't worry: the other basic stitches are easier.

You have now made 1 slip stitch.

STEP 4 Insert the hook under 1 strand of the next chain.

STEP 5 Bring the yarn over the hook and draw through both loops on the hook. Repeat steps 4 and 5, then continue until you have worked into all the stitches of your foundation row. You will have 14 slip stitches. You can see that not much 'height' is created with this stitch.

Once you have got the hang of these two basic stitches – the chain and the slip stitch – you can begin to make projects such as the specs chain, which only uses these two stitches.

The chain
makes a pretty
accessory.

SPECS CHAIN

This simple daisy-chain specs holder makes a great hippy-chic style statement.

Size
The chain can be any length – mine is 90 cm (36 in) long.

Materials
- oddments of any DK yarn (I used Rico Design Essentials Cotton DK, 50 g balls in a selection of shades (130 m/143 yd per ball))
- 1 x 3.5 mm crochet hook (USE/4)
- 8 buttons for flower centres
- specs chain holders – from your local craft store or eBay
- wool sewing needle

Tension
Tension is not important for this project.

Abbreviations
ch = chain
ss = slip stitch
rep = repeat

To make the stem pattern

Row 1: Using a 3.5 mm hook and chosen colour, make a length of 12 ch. * Work leaf as follows: 4 ch, then work ss into fourth ch from hook, work 20 ch, * rep from * to * five more times. Work one more repeat, ending with 13 ch instead of 20 ch.

Row 2: Turn and work back along the length of ch as follows: 1 ss into second ch from hook, 1 ss in each of next 11 ch. * Work leaf as follows: 4 ch, then work ss into fourth ch from hook, then work 1 ss in each of next 20 ch, * rep from * to * ten more times. Work one more repeat, ending with 12 ss instead of 20 ss. Fasten off.

To make the flower (make 8)

Using a 3.5 mm hook and your chosen colour, make a length of 4 ch, join to the first ch with a ss to form a ring. Now work * 6 ch, then 1 ss worked into the ring, rep from * six times in all. Fasten off and cut the yarn, leaving a long end (about 30 cm/12 in) for sewing together.

Making up

Using the long end of yarn left on each daisy, sew one daisy at each end, then sew a daisy halfway between each leaf cluster. Sew buttons into the centre of each daisy. Sew specs holders to each end. Weave in all ends.

The specs chain can be made in any colour combination.

The double crochet stitch

You will have discovered by now that the slip stitch does not add very much height to your work. The double crochet stitch is the first basic stitch that begins to add height, and from which you can begin to make crochet 'fabric' and projects.

A project worked solely in double crochet will be quite solid, so is suitable for items such as bags, jackets and toys. Amigurumi – a Japanese word meaning knitted or crocheted toy – patterns have recently become popular.

Amigurumi toys are cute, hugely popular and are usually worked in double crochet. They can make great beginners' projects. Patterns for these cute creatures can be found on various craft-selling websites.

Amigurumi pattern for an adorable fawn by the very creative Sanda. For sale on her website at www.pepika.com

To make the double crochet (dc)

With a 4 mm hook and any DK yarn, make a length of 15 chain.

STEP 1 Insert the hook from front to back into the top loop of the second chain from the hook. You now have two loops on the hook. **Note:** all subsequent stitches worked into the foundation chain are worked into the *next* chain – omitting the instruction to work into the *second ch from hook*, which only applies to the first stitch worked.

STEP 2 Place the yarn over the hook.

STEP 3 Draw the yarn back through the first loop on the hook. You will still have two loops on the hook.

STEP 4 Place the yarn over the hook again.

STEP 5 Draw the yarn back through both loops on the hook. You will now have only one loop on the hook and you have just completed your first double crochet stitch.

Working into each chain, repeat steps 1 to 5 until you have worked into the last chain. Make sure you don't miss any of the chain stitches. You will now have 14 double crochet stitches and you will notice that there is one chain at the beginning of the row of work. This is called the turning chain.

The first row of double crochet. Now you can work a second row in double crochet.

STEP 1 Turn your work so that the row of stitches to be worked is to the left of the hook.

STEP 2 Work 1 chain. This is the turning chain.

STEP 3 Insert the hook under the top two loops of the first double crochet stitch. Complete the double crochet stitch as given in steps 2 to 5 above. **Note:** The top two loops of the stitch count as one loop on the hook.

STEP 4 Work 1 double crochet into each double crochet of the previous row, until you get to the end. Do not work into the 1 turning chain at the end. You should still have 14 double crochet stitches and 1 turning chain.

Repeat steps 1–4 above to create more rows. Continue like this for a few rows. Fasten off.

TIP

Because there's not a lot to hold on to, the first row of crochet is always the hardest to work and feels awkward. Once you have worked a few rows and there is more to hold, you will find the work becomes easier to manage.

Now you are ready to make a small project. The owl is an ideal project for beginners as it is a simple rectangle made entirely using double crochet stitch. Use a plain, light colour if you are an absolute beginner, so that you can see your stitches better. When you have some more experience you could try using a multicoloured yarn or work the owl using two colours.

OWL BAG CHARM

These whimsical owls make perfect presents.

Size
Approx 9 cm (3½ in) square.

Materials
- oddment of any DK yarn (I used Patons Fab DK in the multicoloured and plain versions (1 x 100 g ball – 274 m/300 yd per ball)

- 1 x 4 mm crochet hook

- 2 x wooden buttons

- small amount of yellow yarn for beak

- small amount of stuffing

- wool sewing needle

- keyring chain

To substitute yarn:
Use correct length of any DK yarn that has a standard knit tension of 22 sts and 28/30 rows to 10 cm square worked on 4 mm (US6) needles.

Tension
The tension for this project is not important, but if you want the owl to be the size given, then after a few rows your work should measure approx 18 cm (7 in) wide. If your work is too small, change to a larger hook and start again; if it is too large, change to a smaller hook and start again.

Abbreviations
ch = chain
dc = double crochet
ss = slip stitch
t-ch = turning chain
rep = repeat

Make the owl

Using a 4 mm hook, make a length of 25 ch and work as follows:

Row 1:   1 dc in 2nd ch from hook (the first 1 ch does *not* count as 1 dc), * 1 dc in next ch, rep from * to end. (24 dc)

Row 2:   1 t-ch (this does *not* count as 1 dc), 1 dc in first dc, * 1 dc in next dc, rep from * to end. (24 dc)

Repeat row 2 until 15 rows have been worked. Fasten off at end of last row.

Making up

Sew buttons for eyes in the centre of the work and approx. 4 rows down from the top edge. Using the photo as a guide, embroider a beak using a few long stitches worked in an upside-down triangle.

With the right sides to the inside, oversew the side edges together to form a tube. Fold the work so that the seam is at the centre back. Oversew the top edge. Turn the work right side out, sew up part of the lower edge and lightly stuff so that most of the stuffing is at the bottom of the owl, and then finish sewing the bottom edge. Sew a keyring chain to the back of the owl.

Make ears (make two)

Thread a long end (approx 2 m/2¼ yd) of the yarn onto a wool sewing needle, pulling it through the eye of the needle so that the yarn is double. Insert needle into top corner of the owl; pull through until approx 4 cm (1½ in) of both ends remain. Make a small backstitch in this position, and then make three more stitches in the same place, each time leaving a long loop of approx 8 cm (3 in); make two more small backstitches in the same position to fix the stitches firmly. Cut the yarn, leaving a 4 cm (1½ in) end. Trim the threads so that they are an even length. Repeat for the other ear.

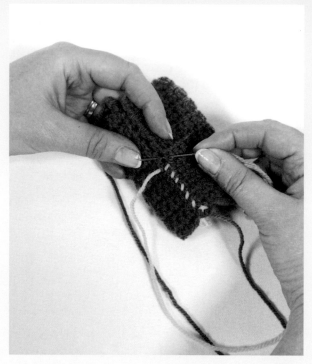

Oversewing the edges together.

Make the owl in two colours

Work as given for the one-colour owl until 9 rows have been worked. At the end of the last row, draw the new colour through the last two loops of the last stitch. (See the instructions for changing colour on page 41.) Cut the end of the old colour, leaving an end to weave in later, and begin the next row using the new colour. Continue until 6 rows of the new colour have been worked. Fasten off and make up as for the one-colour owl.

Your finished owl can be used as a key ring – or it makes a pretty bag charm when attached to a bag.

These owls can be worked in stripes or using multicoloured yarns. A group of owls is called a parliament.

Chapter 3

Changing colours

STEP 1 Work to the stitch before the colour change; complete this stitch until only two loops of the stitch remain to be worked. Bring the yarn over the hook using the new colour.

STEP 2 Draw the new colour through the last two stitches.

STEP 3 Continue working using the new colour yarn.

Starting a new ball of yarn

Larger projects will use more than one ball of yarn. Joining in a new ball of yarn is normally done at the beginning of a row so that the ends can be woven into the seam, however, if you are working something like a scarf that does not have enclosed seams, it is best to join in the middle of the row.

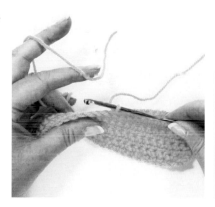

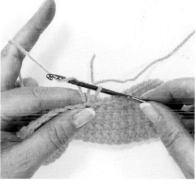

STEP 1 Bring up the new ball of yarn and wind the end round the fingers of your left hand.

STEP 2 Hold the new end of yarn, with the fabric of the work between the thumb and index finger of the left hand, yarn over hook and continue to make the next stitch.

STEP 3 The yarn ends – seen here on the reverse of the work – need to be woven in later.

 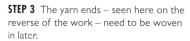

KINDLE CASE

The perfect combination – easy to make, attractive to look at and useful to have.

Size
20.5 cm (8 in) x 13.25 cm
(5¼ in) – this will fit most
e-readers

Materials
- 1 x 100 g ball of James C
  Brett Marble DK shade 29
  (240 m/267 yd per 100 g
  ball)

- 1 x 4 mm crochet hook
  (USG/6)

- 1 large button or toggle

- wool sewing needle

To substitute yarn:
Use correct length of any
DK yarn that has a standard
knit tension of 22 sts and
28/30 rows to 10 cm square
worked on 4 mm (US6) needles.

Tension
After the first few rows
your work should measure
13.25 cm (5¼ in) wide. If your
work is smaller than this, change
to a larger hook and start again;
if it is larger, change to a smaller
hook and start again.

Abbreviations
ch = chain
dc = double crochet
ss = slip stitch
t-ch = turning chain
rep = repeat

The completed e-reader case.

Close-up of the case.

Make the case

Using a 4 mm hook, make a length of 21 ch and work as follows:

Row 1:   1 dc in 2nd ch from hook (the first 1 ch does *not* count as 1 dc), * 1 dc in next ch, rep from * to end. (20 dc)

Row 2:   1 t-ch (this does *not* count as 1 dc), 1 dc in first dc, * 1 dc in next dc, rep from * to end. (20 dc)

Repeat row 2 until 37 rows have been worked in all; place coloured thread for markers in each end of the last row worked, then work 37 more rows and place more coloured thread for markers in each end of the last row worked. Work 16 more rows, then work buttonhole row as follows:

Next row: 1 t-ch (this does *not* count as 1 dc), 1 dc in each of next 8 dc, work 4 ch, skip next 4 dc then work 1 dc in each of rem 8 dc. Fasten off.

Making up

Fold work along first markers so that the first row meets the second set of markers. With right sides together, oversew side seams. Turn right side out so that the oversewing is on the inside. Sew on button to correspond with the loop.

Turning chains

The different crochet stitches have different heights. Some, such as the slip stitch, have hardly any height, whilst others such as the longer trebles have much more.

At the beginning of any row you need to start at the same height as the first stitch of the row. In order to do this a number of chains are worked. These chains produce the required height and usually count as the first stitch of the row. They are called turning chains and the number of chains worked differs from stitch to stitch. Most patterns will give instructions for the turning chains at the beginning of each row, however it is often easier to work them at the end of the last row, before turning the work.

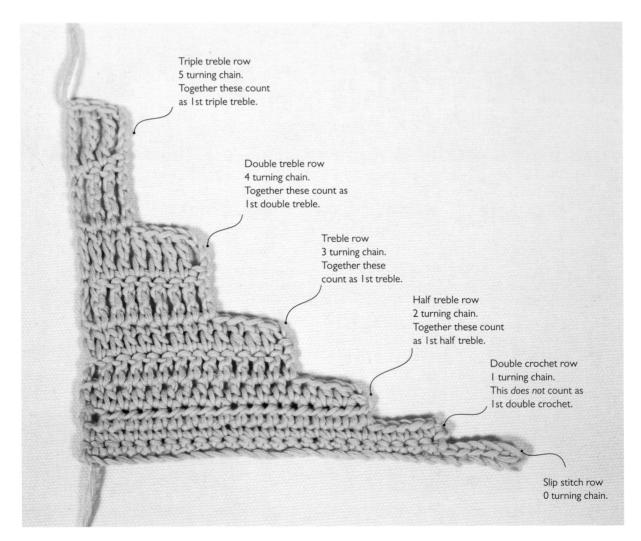

Triple treble row
5 turning chain.
Together these count
as 1st triple treble.

Double treble row
4 turning chain.
Together these count as
1st double treble.

Treble row
3 turning chain.
Together these
count as 1st treble.

Half treble row
2 turning chain.
Together these count
as 1st half treble.

Double crochet row
1 turning chain.
This *does not* count as
1st double crochet.

Slip stitch row
0 turning chain.

You can see that the different basic stitches produce different heights of work, and that each requires a different number of turning chains at the beginning of the row.

Note: The double crochet stitch has a turning chain of 1 chain. This chain does not usually count as a double crochet but is extra to the number of double crochets in the row. Apart from the slip stitch, which does not have a turning chain, all the other basic stitches have turning chains that count as one of the stitches (treble, double treble, etc.) of the row.

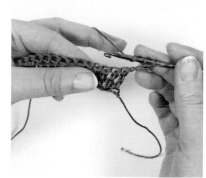

4 turning chain worked at the beginning of a row of double trebles. You can see that the 4 trebles take the place of the first double treble of the row, so the first true double treble is worked in the second stitch of the row.

Keeping edges straight

In order to keep the edges of a piece of work straight, rather than going wobbly or forming a triangle, it is important to understand the rules about these turning chains.

All the stitches apart from the slip stitch and the double crochet have turning chains at the beginning of each row that count as 1 stitch. For these stitches it is important to recognise that the turning chain counts as the first stitch of the row.

When working in rows (rather than in rounds) the stitches are worked into the hole that is slightly to the left of the stitch on the previous row.

Thus, for all the stitches apart from the slip stitch and the double crochet stitch, the first stitch is placed into the hole to the left of the second stitch of the row and the turning chain sits on top of the first stitch of the row and counts as the first

stitch. This can leave a slight gap at the beginning of the row. However, if you try to fill in this gap by working into the first stitch of the row you will actually be making an increase to the number of stitches in your row, causing the edges to slope outwards. If the gap formed by skipping the first stitch is really unsightly it may help if you reduce the number of turning chains used.

At the end of the row, after working into the last true stitch, you will still need to work into the turning chain, which is actually the last stitch of the row. Because all the stitches lean slightly to the left, it may appear as if you are making an increase as this last stitch seems to hang off the edge of the work. If you make the mistake of not working into this last stitch because it doesn't look right, you will find that the number of stitches gradually decreases and your edges will slope inwards.

The stitches are worked into the hole that is slightly to the left of the stitch on the previous row.

The half treble stitch

The half treble stitch makes a taller stitch and like the double crochet stitch is often used for bulky projects such as coats, hats, scarves and bags.

To make the half treble (htr)

With a 4 mm hook and any DK yarn, make a length of 15 chain.

STEP 1 Place the yarn over the hook.

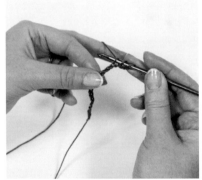

STEP 2 Insert the hook from front to back into the top loop of the third chain from the hook. You now have three loops on the hook. **Note:** all subsequent stitches worked into the foundation chain are worked into the *next* chain – omitting the instruction to work into the *third ch from hook*, which only applies to the first stitch worked.

STEP 3 Place the yarn over the hook.

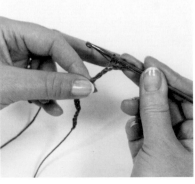

STEP 4 Draw the yarn back through the first loop on the hook. You will still have three loops on the hook.

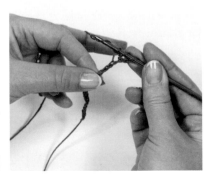

STEP 5 Place the yarn over the hook again.

Working into each chain, repeat steps 1 to 6 until you have worked into the last chain. Make sure you don't miss any of the chain stitches. You will now have 13 half treble stitches and there are two chain stitches at the beginning of the row. These two chains are called the turning chain and they count as a half treble.

STEP 6 Draw the yarn back through all three loops on the hook. You have now completed your first half treble stitch.

Now you can work a second row in half trebles.

STEP 1 Turn the work so that the row of stitches to be worked is to the left of the hook.

STEP 2 Work 2 chain. These are the turning chain – they count as 1 half treble.

STEP 3 Place the yarn over the hook and then insert the hook under the top two loops of the second half treble stitch – counting in from the end of the previous row. (The top two loops of the stitch count as one loop on the hook.) Complete the half treble stitch as given in steps 3 to 6 above.

STEP 4 Work 1 half treble into each half treble of the previous row, until you get to the end, then work 1 half treble into the second of the 2 turning chain. You should still have 14 half treble stitches counting the 2 turning chain as 1 half treble.

Repeat the four steps above to create more rows. Fasten off.

PIXIE HOOD

Warm, practical and pretty, this pixie hood is worked in half trebles and also introduces you to working an edging.

Size

23 cm (9 in) wide x 24 cm (9½ in) deep – suitable for a child aged 4–6 years

Materials

- 1 x 100 g ball of King Cole Riot Chunky in shade Dawn 652 (134 m/147 yd per 100 g ball)

- 1 x 6 mm crochet hook (USJ/10)

- small piece of cardboard

- wool sewing needle

To substitute yarn:

Use correct length of any chunky yarn that has a standard knit tension of 14 sts and 20 rows to 10 cm square worked on 6 mm (US10) needles.

Tension

Using a 6 mm hook, 12 htr and 9 rows should measure 10 cm (4 in) square. When you have worked the first few rows the work should measure 21.5 cm (8½ in) across. In order for the hood to be the size given you will need to achieve this tension. If your work is too small, change to a larger hook and start again; if it is too large, change to a smaller hook and start again.

Abbreviations

ch = chain
htr = half treble
t-ch = turning chain
rep = repeat

Close-up of the pixie hood.

Make the hood

With a 6 mm hook, make a length of 57 ch.

Row 1: 1 htr in third ch from hook (the first 2 ch count as 1 htr), 1 htr in each of the next 24 ch (26 htr). Turn, leaving 30 ch unworked.

Row 2: 2 t-ch (counts as 1 htr), skip first htr, * 1 htr in next htr, rep from * to end, working the last htr in the second of 2 t-ch (26 htr).

Repeat row 2 until there are 43 rows. Work a length of 31 ch (this will be at the same edge of the work as the first length of 30 ch).

Work border

Next row: 1 htr into third ch from hook (the first 2 ch count as 1 htr), 1 htr into each remaining 28 ch to beginning of hood, work 56 htr evenly along row ends of hood (see instructions below), work 30 htr in remaining length of 30 ch. Fasten off (116 htr).

Making up

Fold work in half lengthways, so that the right side is on the inside. Oversew the long edge that has no border. Weave in all ends. Turn right sides out.

Make three tassels as shown on page 51, and using the long ends of yarn on each tassel, sew a tassel to the end of each tie and one to the back corner of the hood.

Working into the side edges of a piece of work

STEP 1 Insert the hook into the main work at the starting point for the edging. It's usually best to push the hook through the strands of the yarn as this makes the edge firmer and less holey.

STEP 2 Leaving a long end of yarn to weave in later, bring the yarn for the edging over the hook. (Here I am using a contrasting colour.)

STEP 3 Draw the yarn through the work, forming a loop on the hook.

STEP 4 Work the required number of turning chain. This depends on the stitch to be used. Here I have worked 2 chain stitches for an edging to be worked in half trebles.

STEP 5 Work the next stitch, inserting the hook back into the edge of the main work.

STEP 6 Continue to work stitches into the edge of the main work. For the pixie hood you will need to work approximately 12 half trebles into every 9 rows – or 10 cm.

TIP

Your pattern will usually give the number of stitches to be worked along the edge. It is a good idea to divide up the edge, placing markers along, and then divide the number of stitches to be worked by the number of sections. Work the correct number of stitches in each section in order to create evenly placed edging stitches.

How to make a tassel

STEP 1 Cut a piece of card approximately 10 cm (4 in) square.

STEP 2 Wind yarn around this card about 14 times (wind the same amount for each tassel) and cut the yarn.

STEP 3 Cut a length of yarn from the ball and thread this onto a sewing needle.

STEP 4 Pass this under all the wrapped yarn at one edge and knot securely, leaving long ends of yarn.

STEP 5 Cut the opposite edge.

STEP 6 Wind yarn around the top of the tassel and knot together.

STEP 7 Thread the yarn ends onto the needle and pass down into the tassel.

STEP 8 Cut the ends of the yarn so that they are all the same length. If the yarn is a bit curly you can hold the tassel near the steam from a kettle and the kinks will drop out. Take care when doing this, as steam can scald.

COASTERS

These coasters are perfect for colour co-ordinated parties. Make them with plain or contrasting edges.

Size
9 cm (3½ in) square

Materials
- 1 x 50 g ball each of Rowan Cotton Glacé in shades Persimmon 832, Mineral 856, and Shoot 814 (115 m/126 yd per 50 g ball)

- 1 x 3.5 mm crochet hook (USE/4)

- wool sewing needle

To substitute yarn:
Use correct length of any DK yarn that has a standard knit tension of 22 sts and 28/30 rows to 10 cm square worked on 4 mm (US6) needles.

Tension
Although this is a DK weight yarn I have used a smaller hook to make the coasters more robust.

In order for the coaster to be the size given, you will need to work to a tension of 17 half trebles and 14 rows to 10 cm (4 in) square. Check your tension by working a few rows of the pattern: the work should measure 8 cm (3¼ in) across. If your work is too small, change to a larger hook and start again; if it is too large, change to a smaller hook and start again.

Abbreviations
beg = beginning
ch = chain
htr = half treble
prev = previous
rep = repeat
ss = slip stitch
t-ch = turning chain

Make the coaster

With a 3.5 mm hook, make a length of 15 ch.

Row 1:   1 htr into third ch from hook (first 2 ch count as 1 htr) *1 htr into next ch, rep from * to end (14 htr).

Row 2   2 t-ch (counts as 1 htr), skip 1st htr, * 1 htr in next htr, rep from * to end, working the last htr in second of 2 t-ch (14 htr).

Repeat row 2 until there are 11 rows in all. The work should now be square. Adjust the number of rows if necessary, to create a square. Follow the instructions below to create the border.

Border

Next row: 2 t-ch (counts as 1 htr). Skip first htr of row (this is the last htr of prev row), (1 htr in next htr) x 12, 3 htr in second of 2 ch at beg of prev row, then working into the row ends of the side edge, work 12 htr to corner. Now working along the ch edge at beg of work, work 3 htr into the first ch, then work 1 htr in each of next 12 ch, work 3 tr in next ch, then working into the row ends of the next side edge, work 12 htr to corner. Work 2 htr into base of first 2 t-ch of round, and join to second of these 2 t-ch with a ss. Fasten off and weave in all ends.

The coaster.

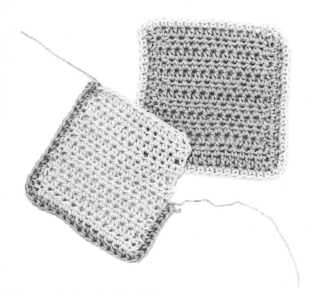

You can work the border in a contrasting colour, however working this straight into the edges can leave a rather untidy edge. (See the coaster with the blue edge being worked.) For a neater contrasting border, work 1 row of edging in the main colour and then 1 row of edging in the contrast colour (as in the coaster with the yellow edge).

The treble stitch

The treble stitch makes a taller stitch and is probably the most used of all the crochet stitches.

To make the treble (tr)

With a 4 mm hook and any DK yarn, make a length of 16 chain.

STEP 1 Place the yarn over the hook.

STEP 2 Insert the hook from front to back into the top loop of the fourth chain from the hook. You now have three loops on the hook. **Note:** all subsequent stitches worked into the foundation chain are worked into the *next* chain – omitting the instruction to work into the *fourth ch from hook*, which only applies to the first stitch worked.

STEP 3 Place the yarn over the hook.

STEP 4 Draw the yarn back through the first loop on the hook. You will have three loops on the hook.

STEP 5 Place the yarn over the hook again.

STEP 6 Draw the yarn back through the first two loops on the hook. There are now two loops on the hook.

STEP 7 Place the yarn over the hook again.

STEP 8 Draw the yarn back through the two loops on the hook. This completes the treble stitch. Working into each chain, repeat steps 1 to 8 until you have worked into the last chain. Make sure you don't miss any of the chain stitches. You will now have 13 treble stitches. There are 3 chain stitches at the beginning of the row of work: these are called the turning chain and they count as 1 treble.

Now you can work a second row of trebles.

STEP 1 Turn the piece of work so that the row of stitches to be worked is to the left of the hook.

STEP 2 Work 3 chain. These are the turning chains – they count as 1 treble.

STEP 3 Place the yarn over the hook, then insert the hook under the top two loops of the second treble stitch – counting in from the end – of the previous row. (The top two loops of the stitch count as one loop on the hook.) Complete the treble stitch as shown in steps 3 to 8 above.

STEP 4 Work one treble into each treble of the previous row until you get to the end, then work one treble into the third of the 3 turning chain. You should still have 14 treble stitches counting the 3 turning chain as 1 treble.

Repeat the four steps above to create more rows. Fasten off.

FINGERLESS GLOVES

Simple treble gloves to keep you warm when you're working. They are worked using the treble stitch and are joined at the side seam. Easy to work, they are an ideal practical beginner's project, and make a great present.

Size
22 cm (8¾ in) long x 22 cm (8¾ in) round (with some stretch) when finished – will fit most adults

Materials
- 2 x 50 g ball of King Cole Baby Alpaca shade 502 Grey (100 m/110 yd per 50 g ball)

- 1 x 4 mm crochet hook (USG/6)

- wool sewing needle

To substitute yarn:
Use correct length of any DK yarn that has a standard knit tension of 22 sts and 28/30 rows to 10 cm square worked on 4 mm (US6) needles.

Tension
In order for the gloves to be the size given you will need to work to a tension of 16 trebles and 9 rows to 10 cm (4 in) square. After a few rows you can check the width, which should be 22 cm. If your work is too small, change to a larger hook and start again; if it is too large, change to a smaller hook and start again.

Abbreviations
ch = chain
rep = repeat
t-ch = turning chain
tr = treble

The fingerless gloves are great for working outside on cold days.

Make the gloves (make two)

Using a 4 mm hook and leaving a long end of yarn (about 30 cm), make a length of 37 ch and work as follows:

Row 1:   1 tr in fourth ch from hook (the first 3 ch count as 1 tr), * 1 tr in next ch, rep from * to end (35 tr).

Row 2:   3 t-ch (counts as 1 tr), skip first tr, * 1 tr in next tr, rep from * to end, working last tr in third of 3 t-ch (35 tr).

Rep row 2 until 20 rows have been worked. Fasten off at end of the last row, leaving a long end of yarn (about 30 cm/12 in).

Making up

Thread the long end of yarn from the end of the work onto a wool sewing needle and oversew the side edges of the work together – so that the work lies flat when opened out – sewing the first nine rows only. Then fasten off and weave in the end. Thread the long end of yarn from the beginning of the work onto a wool sewing needle and oversew the side edges of the work together – so that the work lies flat when opened out – sewing the first six rows only. Then fasten off and weave in the ends. This will leave a gap of five rows for the thumb.

The finished gloves.

TIP
The length of these gloves can be adjusted by working more or fewer rows than stated in the pattern.

THE CROCHET COWL

This classic cowl should be a standard item for everyone's winter wardrobe. Made entirely from trebles, its interest comes from the luxurious hand-dyed yarn.

Size

Small/medium and medium/large, 96[108] cm (37¾[42½] in) around and 35[40] cm (13¾[15¾] in) deep. **Note:** Figures in square brackets refer to the larger size. Where the instructions give only one number, this applies to both sizes.

Materials

- 3[4] 100 g hanks of Colinette Art shade 176 Adonis Blue (173 m/190 yd per 100 g ball) **Note:** This yarn comes in hanks and you will need to wind it into a ball.

- 1 x 5 mm crochet hook (USH/8)

- wool sewing needle

To substitute yarn:

Use correct length of any Aran weight yarn that has a standard knit tension of 19 sts and 24 rows to 10 cm square worked on 5 mm (US8) needles.

Tension

Although the tension is not critical, in order for the cowl to be the size given you will need to work to a tension of 14 tr and 8 rows to 10 cm (4 in) square. When you have worked the first few rows of the cowl the work should measure 96 [108] cm wide. If your work is too small, change to a larger hook and start again; if it is too large, change to a smaller hook and start again.

Abbreviations

ch = chain
rep = repeat
t-ch = turning chain
tr = treble

Make the cowl

Using a 5 mm hook, make a length of 137[154] ch.

Row 1: 1 tr in fourth ch from hook (the first 3 ch count as 1 tr), * 1 tr in next ch, rep from * to end (135[152] tr).

Row 2: 3 t-ch (counts as 1 tr) skip first tr, * 1 tr in next tr, rep from * to end, working last tr in third of 3 t-ch (135[152] tr).

Rep row 2 until work measures 35[40] cm (13¾[15¾] in). Fasten off.

Making up

Weave in all ends and join the short edges by oversewing so that the work lies flat when opened out.

TIP

If you don't have a willing pair of hands to hold the yarn while you wind it into a ball, you can place the hank on an upside-down washing basket.

TIP

When making a garment the widthways tension (the number of stitches) is usually more important than the lengthways tension, as the number of rows can be adjusted when working.

Close-up of the yarn and stitches.

The finished cowl can be worn over the head or around the neck.

The longer treble stitches

The treble stitch can be made much longer. These longer trebles form a weak fabric when worked on their own, but often form part of various crochet stitch patterns. Longer treble stitches are called double treble and triple treble, but they can be made even longer. They are all worked in the same way as the treble stitch but with more loops.

To make the double treble (dtr)

With a 4 mm hook and any DK yarn, make a length of 17 chain.

STEP 1 Place the yarn over the hook twice.

STEP 2 Insert the hook from front to back into the top loop of the fifth chain from the hook. You now have four loops on the hook. **Note:** all subsequent stitches worked into the foundation chain are worked into the *next* chain – omitting the instruction to work into the *fifth ch from hook*, which only applies to the first stitch worked.

STEP 3 Place the yarn over the hook.

STEP 4 Draw the yarn back through the first loop on the hook. You will have four loops on the hook.

STEP 5 Place the yarn over the hook again.

STEP 6 Draw the yarn back through the first two loops on the hook. There are now three loops on the hook.

STEP 7 Place the yarn over the hook again.

STEP 8 Draw the yarn back through the first two loops on the hook. There are now two loops on the hook.

STEP 9 Place the yarn over the hook again.

STEP 10 Draw the yarn back through the last two loops on the hook. This completes the double treble stitch. Working into each chain, repeat steps 1 to 10 until you have worked into the last chain. Make sure you don't miss any of the chain stitches. You will now have 13 double treble stitches and there are 4 chain at the beginning of the row of work. These 4 chains are called the turning chain and they count as 1 double treble.

Now you can work a second row of double trebles.

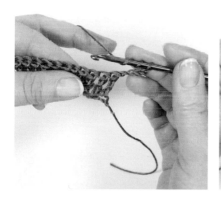

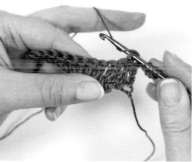

STEP 1 Turn the piece of work so that the row of stitches to be worked is to the left of the hook.

STEP 2 Work 4 chain. These are the turning chain – they count as 1 double treble.

STEP 3 Place the yarn over the hook twice and then insert the hook under the top two loops of the second double treble stitch – counting in from the end – of the previous row. (The top two loops of the stitch count as 1 loop on the hook.) Complete the double treble stitch as given in steps 3 to 10 above.

STEP 4 Work 1 double treble into each double treble of the previous row, until you get to the end, work 1 double treble into the fourth of the 4 turning chain. You should still have 14 double trebles, counting the 4 turning chain as 1 double treble.

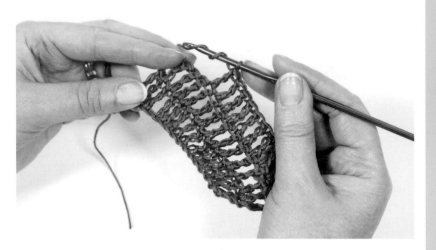

Repeat these four steps to create more rows. Fasten off.

To make the triple treble

With a 4 mm hook and any DK yarn, make a length of 18 chain.

STEP 1 Place the yarn over the hook three times.

STEP 2 Insert the hook from front to back into the top loop of the sixth chain from the hook. You now have five loops on the hook. **Note:** all subsequent stitches worked into the foundation chain are worked into the *next* chain – omitting the instruction to work into the *sixth ch from hook*, which only applies to the first stitch worked.

STEP 3 Place the yarn over the hook.

STEP 4 Draw the yarn back through the first loop on the hook. You will have five loops on the hook.

STEP 5 Place the yarn over the hook again.

Now you can work a second row of triple trebles.

STEP 6 Draw the yarn back through the first two loops on the hook. Repeat steps 5 and 6 three more times. One loop is left on the hook and you have just completed the first triple treble.

Working into each chain, repeat steps 1 to 6 until you have worked into the last chain. Make sure you don't miss any of the chain stitches. You will now have 13 triple treble stitches and there are 5 chain at the beginning of the row of work. These 5 chains are called the turning chain and they count as one triple treble.

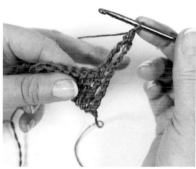

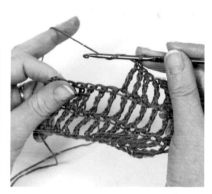

STEP 1 Turn the work so that the row of stitches to be worked is to the left of the hook.

STEP 2 Work 5 chain. These are the turning chain – they count as 1 triple treble.

STEP 3 Place the yarn over the hook three times.

STEP 4 Complete the triple treble stitch as given in steps 3 to 6 above.

STEP 5 Work 1 triple treble into each triple treble of the previous row, until you get to the end, work one triple treble into the fifth of the 5 turning chain. You should still have 14 triple treble stitches, counting the 5 turning chain as 1 triple treble.

Repeat the five steps above to create more rows. Fasten off.

Even longer trebles

The quadruple treble is made as follows: place the yarn over the hook four times at the beginning of the stitch, work steps 1 to 4 as given for the triple treble, then repeat steps 5 and 6 four more times. Even longer stitches can be made in this same way.

LONG TREBLE SCARVES

These bright scarves bring a burst of colour to wintry days.

Size

13.5 cm (5¼ in) wide and 125 cm (49¼ in) long (not including the bobble) – suitable for a child aged about 5–8 years

Materials

For the scarf worked in double trebles:

- 1 x 100 g ball each of Hayfield Baby DK in shades Pretty Little Lemon 452 and Truly Turquoise (350 m/383 yd per ball)

For the scarf worked in triple trebles:

- 1 x 100 g ball each of Hayfield Baby DK in shades Eyepopping Pink 461 and Limelight 462 (350 m/383 yd per ball)

For both scarves:

- 1 x 4 mm crochet hook (USG/6)

- cardboard from an old cereal packet to make the pompom, or a Clover Pompom Maker (large size – 8.5 cm / 3⅜ in) from your local yarn store or eBay

- wool sewing needle

To substitute yarn:

Use any DK yarn that has a standard knit tension of 22 sts and 28/30 rows to 10 cm square worked on 4 mm (US6) needles.

Tension

Tension is not important for this project, but to achieve the same measurements as the scarves shown in the photo you should work to the following tensions:

- for the double treble scarf – 15 dtr and 6½ rows to 10 cm square

- for the triple treble scarf – 15 dtr and 4½ rows to 10 cm square.

When you have worked the first few rows the work should measure approx 13.5 cm (5¼ in) across the width. In order for the scarves to be the size given you will need to achieve this tension. If your work is too small, change to a larger hook and start again; if it is too large, change to a smaller hook and start again.

Abbreviations

ch = chain
dtr = double treble
rep = repeat
t-ch = turning chain
ttr = triple treble

Close-up of the double treble scarf.

Make the double treble scarf

Using a 4 mm hook and yellow yarn, leave a long end of yarn (about 30 cm) and make a length of 23 ch. Now work as follows:

Row 1: 1 dtr in 5th ch from hook (the first 4 ch count as 1 dtr), * 1 dtr in next ch, rep from * to end (20 dtr).

Row 2: 4 t-ch (counts as 1 dtr), skip 1st dtr (this is the last dtr of previous row), * 1 dtr in next dtr, rep from * to end, working last dtr in 4th of 4 t-ch that form the 1st dtr of previous row (20 dtr).

Rep row 2 until work measures 125 cm – or any length you like – then fasten off, leaving a long end of yarn (about 30 cm).

Close-up of the triple treble scarf.

Making up

Thread the long yarn end onto a wool sewing needle and sew in and out of the edge stitches; pull to gather up the edge and sew into place to fix the gathers, then weave in the yarn end and cut off. Work the other edge in the same way. Using the turquoise yarn, make pompoms following the instructions given on page 67 or 68, and sew firmly onto each end of the scarf.

Make the triple treble scarf

Using a 4 mm hook and pink yarn, leave a long end of yarn (about 30 cm) and then make a length of 24 ch. Now work as follows:

Row 1: 1 ttr in 6th ch from hook (the first 5 ch count as 1 ttr), * 1 ttr in next ch, rep from * to end (20 ttr).

Row 2: 5 t-ch (counts as 1 ttr), skip 1st ttr (this is the last ttr of previous row), * 1 ttr in next ttr, rep from * to end, working last ttr in 5th of 5 t-ch that form the 1st ttr of previous row (20 ttr).

Rep row 2 until work measures 125 cm – or any length you like – then fasten off, leaving a long end of yarn (about 30 cm).

Making up

Make up as for the double treble scarf, working the pompoms in green.

Wear two scarves at a time for impact.

To make pompoms using cardboard

STEP 1 Using the cardboard from an old cereal packet – or similar – and compasses or a round object such as a mug, draw a circle with a diameter of approximately 8 cm.

STEP 2 Draw a smaller circle – diameter 3 cm – in the centre of this circle.

STEP 3 Cut around these circles so that you have a doughnut shape, then make another the same.

STEP 4 Place the two rings together.

STEP 5 Cut the wool into manageable lengths of about 1 m, then wind the yarn around the doughnut as shown in the photo. Continue until the centre is filled. You don't need to knot the lengths of yarn together as you go.

STEP 6 Insert the point of the scissors into the wool at the edge so that it slides between the two layers of cardboard, and cut through the yarn round the edge.

STEP 7 Open out the layers of cardboard a little and wrap a length of yarn around the middle. Tie it tightly so that all the yarns are held together firmly. Do not cut off the ends of the yarn.

STEP 8 Remove the cardboard and, taking care not to cut the ends of the tie, trim any uneven bits of wool so that the pompom is nice and round without any bits sticking out.

Thread the ends of the tie onto a needle and sew onto the end of the scarf.

Pompom maker made by Clover. These come in various sizes for different sized pompoms. Although they look complicated, they are easy to use and the packet gives clear instructions.

To make pompoms using a pompom maker

Using a commercial pompom maker is quicker and easier than the traditional method given above, although it does tend to make a looser pompom.

THE SHOPPING BAG

This lightweight bag packs up small into your pocket but will expand with your shopping.
The pattern uses a variety of basic stitches and introduces simple increases and decreases.

Size
Approx 70 cm (27½ in) deep
(including handles) and 38 cm
(15 in) wide

Materials
• 2 x DMC Natura Just Cotton
50 g balls (155 m/170 yd) in
shade Paille N42, Safran N47 and
Turquoise N49

• 3.5 mm crochet hook (USE/4)

• wool sewing needle

To substitute yarn:
Use correct length of any 4 ply yarn
that has a knit tension of 27 sts and
34 rows to 10 cm square worked on
3.5 mm (US4) needles.

Tension
Tension is not vital, but to achieve
the size given, the triple treble grid
should measure 4½ x 4 pattern
repeats to 10 cm (4 in). If your work
is too small, change to a larger hook;
if it is too large, change to a smaller
hook.

Abbreviations
beg = beginning
ch = chain
cont = continue
dtr = double treble
htr = half treble
htr 2 tog = * yoh, insert hook into
st, yoh, draw through, * yoh draw
through two loops, working into next
st, rep from * to * once, yoh, draw
through all four loops on the hook.
These 2 sts now count as 1 st
rem = remaining
rep = repeat
RS = right side
sp = space
st = stitch
t-ch = turning chain
ttr = triple treble
yoh = yarn over hook

The shopping bag:
put one in your suitcase
to take on holiday for
all your beach stuff.

Make the bag

Using a 3.5 mm hook, make a length of 32 ch
and work as follows:

Row 1: 1 dtr in 5th ch from hook, * 2 dtr in next
ch, 1 dtr in each of next 2 ch, rep from
* to last ch, 1 dtr in last ch. Turn. (38 dtr
counting 1st 4 ch as 1 dtr)

Row 2: 4 t-ch (counts as 1 dtr), skip 1st dtr of
row, * 1 ch, 1 dtr in next dtr, rep from * to
end, working last dtr into the 4th of 4 t-ch
at beg of previous row. Turn. (38 dtr and
37 ch sp)

Row 3: 5 t-ch (counts as 1 ttr), skip 1st dtr of
row, * 2 ch, 1 ttr in next dtr, rep from * to
end, working last ttr into the 4th of 4 t-ch
at beg of previous row. Turn. (38 ttr and
37 ch sp)

Row 4: 5 t-ch, (counts as 1 ttr), skip 1st ttr of
row, * 4 ch, 1 ttr in next ttr, rep from * to
end, working last ttr into the 5th of 5 t-ch
at beg of previous row. Turn. (38 ttr and
37 ch sp)

The fourth row forms the pattern. Rep row 4 for
another 14 rows.

Row 19: 5 t-ch (counts as 1 ttr), skip 1st ttr of row,
* 2 ch, 1 ttr in next ttr, rep from * to end,
working last ttr into the 5th of 5 t-ch at
beg of previous row. Turn. (38 ttr and
37 ch sp)

Row 20: 2 t-ch (counts as 1 htr), skip 1st ttr of row,
* 2 htr in next 2 ch sp, 1 htr in next ttr, rep
from * to end, working last htr into the
5th of 5 t-ch at beg of previous row. Turn.
(112 htr)

Row 21: 2 t-ch (counts as 1 htr), skip 1st htr of row,
* 1 htr in each htr to end of row, working
last htr in 2 t-ch at end of row. Turn.
(112 htr)

Rep row 21 eight more times. Fasten off.

Handles

With RS facing, count 14 htr in from side seam and
rejoin yarn to next htr with a ss.

**

Row 1: 2 t-ch (counts as 1 htr), htr 2 tog in
next 2 htr, 1 htr in each of next 22 htr,
htr 2 tog, 1 htr in next htr. Turn. (26 htr)

Row 2: 2 t-ch (counts as 1 htr), skip 1st htr, htr
2 tog in next 2 htr, 1 htr in each htr to
last 3 htr, htr 2 tog, 1 htr in 2 t-ch at end
of row. Turn. (24 htr)

Rep row 2 five more times. Then cont working rows
of half treble on the rem 14 sts for 20 more rows.
Fasten off.
**

With RS facing, count 28 htr in from first handle
and rejoin yarn to next st with a ss.
Work second handle to match first as given
from ** to **.

Making up

Press the bag if necessary, then, with right sides
together, pin the sides of the bag together and
oversew them so that the work lies flat when opened
out. Oversew the last row of the handles together.
Weave in all ends. Turn right side out.

TIP

Some of the increases in the
bag are worked by adding
chain stitches between the
double trebles. The decreases
are worked by reducing the
number of chain stitches
between the double trebles.
This is a very simple way to
introduce shaping.

Visit the local farmers' market and fill your bag with yummy fruit and veg.

Chapter 6

Stitch patterns

7

Crochet is a truly flexible craft. Having learnt the basic stitches: slip stitch, double crochet, half treble, treble, double treble and the longer treble variations, you are fully equipped to move on to create stitch patterns. Crochet stitch patterns make use of the basic stitches by combining and using them in different ways to make an infinite variety of patterns. You don't need to be frightened by shells and puffs, popcorn and clusters, as you already know how to make the stitches from which they are formed.

MULTIPLES

Because all stitch patterns make use of combinations of several stitches, the starting length of chain needs to be a multiple of the number of these stitches. Often added to this multiple are a few extra stitches at the beginning and end of the row. So for example, the stitch pattern for the purple pot holder given on the next page is worked over a multiple of two stitches with two extra stitches added to the foundation chain. The two extra stitches are for one turning chain and one extra stitch to balance the pattern.

The next few pages will show examples of various stitch patterns. These will all happily make potholders or table mats so that your worked examples can have some purpose too.

TIP

Crochet terms such as 'puff' or 'popcorn' are not standardised and may differ from pattern to pattern. You will need to check the list of abbreviations for each of these terms to check that you are working the stitch correctly.

SIMPLE TEXTURED STITCH PATTERNS:

TEXTURED POT HOLDERS

These simple pot holders make great Christmas presents.

Size
Approx 16 cm (6¼ in) square

Materials
For each pot holder you will need:

- 1 x 50 g ball King Cole Merino Blend DK in shades 787 Fuchsia and 788 Bilberry (112 m/123 yd per 50 g ball)

- 1 x 4 mm crochet hook (USG/6)

- wool sewing needle

To substitute yarn:
Use correct length of any DK yarn that has a standard knit tension of 22 sts and 28/30 rows to 10 cm square worked on 4 mm (US6) needles.

Tension
The tension for this project is not important, but if you want the pot holders to be the size given, then after a few rows your work should measure approx 16 cm (6 in) wide. If your work is too small, change to a larger hook and start again; if it is too large, change to a smaller hook and start again.

Abbreviations
ch = chain
dc = double crochet
htr = half treble
rep = repeat
st = stitch
t-ch = turning chain
tr = treble

Make the pink pot holder

Using a 4 mm hook, make a length of 28 ch and work as follows:

Row 1: 1 tr in 4th ch from hook (the first 3 ch count as 1 tr), *1 tr in next ch, rep from * to end (26 tr).

Row 2: 3 t-ch (counts as 1 tr), * 1 tr in next tr, working into the back loop only of each stitch, rep from * working last tr into 3rd of 3 t-ch (26 tr).

Repeat row 2 until 14 rows have been worked, or until work forms a square.

Row 15: 2 t-ch (counts as 1 htr), * 1 htr in next tr, rep from * to last st, 1 htr in 3rd of 3 t-ch. Work 20 ch for hanging loop, work 1 htr back into 3rd of 3 t-ch.

Edging

Work 23 htr along side edge to corner, work 3 htr in corner, work 23 htr along foundation ch at bottom edge, work 3 htr in next corner, work 23 htr along 2nd side edge, work 2 htr back into base of 1st 2 t-ch of 15th row, ss to 2nd of 2 t-ch. Fasten off and weave in all ends.

Close-up of the pot holder. This stitch pattern can be worked over any number of stitches.

Make the purple pot holder

For this stitch pattern you will need a length of chain with a multiple of 2 sts + 2 sts.

Using a 4 mm hook, make a length of 26 ch and work as follows:

Row 1: 1 dc in 2nd ch from hook (the first 1 ch does not count as 1 dc), * 1 tr in next ch, 1 dc in next ch, rep from * to end (25 sts).

Row 2: 3 t-ch (counts as 1st tr), * 1 dc in next tr, 1 tr in next dc, rep from * to end (25 sts).

Row 3: 1 t-ch (does not count as 1st dc), 1 dc in first tr, * 1 tr in next dc, 1 dc in next tr, rep from * working last dc in 3rd of 3 t-ch (25 sts).

Rows 2 and 3 form the pattern. Continue in pattern until 23 rows have been worked or until work forms a square.

Row 24: 2 t-ch (counts as 1 htr), * 1 htr in next st, rep from * to end of row. Work 20 ch for hanging loop, work 1 htr back into last st.

Edging

Work 23 htr along side edge to corner, work 3 htr in corner, work 23 htr along foundation ch at bottom edge, work 3 htr in next corner, work 23 htr along 2nd side edge, work 2 htr back into base of 1st 2 t-ch of 15th row, ss to 2nd of 2 t-ch. Fasten off and weave in all ends.

Close-up of the pot holder.

MUG WARMERS IN SHELL STITCH PATTERN

This pretty shell stitch mug warmer will keep your coffee warm.

Size

25 cm (10 in) wide x 7.5 cm (3 in) deep, including edging – fits a mug of 26 cm (10¼ in) circumference

Materials

- 1 x 50 g ball each of Rico Creative Cotton Aran in shades 80 White, 64 Candy Pink or 16 Violet (use all three colours for the three-coloured version) (85 m/95 yd per 50 g ball)

- 1 x 4.5 mm crochet hook (US nearest equivalent H/8)

- 1 large button

- wool sewing needle

To substitute yarn:

Use correct length of any Aran weight yarn that has a standard knit tension of 18 sts and 24 rows to 10 cm square worked on 5 mm (US8) needles.

Tension

When you have worked the first few rows, the work should measure 24 cm (9½ in) wide. In order for the mug warmer to be the size given you will need to achieve this measurement. If your work is too small, change to a larger hook and start again; if it is too large, change to a smaller hook and start again

Abbreviations

ch = chain
dc = double crochet
rep = repeat
shell = work 5 tr into one stitch
st = stitch
t-ch = turning chain
tr = treble

Make the mug warmer in one colour

You will need a length of chain with a multiple of 6 sts + 2 sts + turning chain.
Using a 4.5 mm hook, make a length of 39 chain and work as follows:

Row 1:   1 dc in 3rd ch from hook, * skip 2 ch, work shell into next ch, skip 2 ch, 1 dc in next ch, rep from * to end (6 shells).

Row 2:   3 t-ch (counts as 1 tr), 2 tr in first dc, * 1 dc in centre tr of next shell, work shell in next dc, rep from * to last repeat. Work last rep: 1 dc in centre tr of next shell, work 3 tr in last dc.

Row 3:   1 ch, 1 dc in first tr of row, * work shell in next dc, 1 dc in centre tr of next shell, rep from * work last dc into 3rd of 3 t-ch.

Rep rows 2 and 3 twice more. Do not cut yarn but work edge as follows:

Edge

Row 1:   2 t-ch (counts as 1 dc), working into the side edge work 9 dc to corner, work 3 dc in corner then working along foundation ch work 36 dc to next corner, work 3 dc in corner, then working along 2nd side edge work 4 dc, 10 ch, skip 1 cm of the edge then work 4 dc in remainder of edge. Fasten off.

Making up

Weave in all ends. Sew button to middle of side edge to correspond with button loop and to fit mug.

Make the mug warmer in three colours

Using a 4.5 mm hook and pink yarn, make a length of 39 chain and work as follows:

Row 1:   1 dc in 3rd ch from hook (1st 2 ch count as 1 dc) * skip 2 ch, work shell into next ch, skip 2 ch, 1 dc in next ch, rep from * to end drawing white yarn through last 2 loops worked (6 shells).

Row 2:   With white yarn, 3 t-ch (counts as 1 tr), 2 tr in first dc, * 1 dc in centre tr of next shell, work shell in next dc, rep from * to last repeat. Work last rep: 1 dc in centre tr of next shell, work 3 tr in 2nd of 2 t-ch, drawing violet yarn through last 2 loops worked. Turn and do not cut the white yarn.

Row 3:   With violet yarn, 1 ch, 1 dc in first tr, * work shell in next dc, 1 dc in centre tr of next shell, rep from *, working last dc into 3rd of 3 t-ch and drawing pink yarn through last 2 loops worked. Turn and do not cut the violet yarn.

Keeping continuity of colour sequence and bringing the yarn loosely up the side edge before starting each row, rep rows 2 and 3 twice more. Do not cut yarn but work edge as follows:

Edge

Row 1:   2 t-ch (counts as 1 dc), working into the side edge, and enclosing the strands of yarn at side edge, work 8 dc to corner, work 3 dc in corner then working along foundation ch work 36 dc to next corner, work 3 dc in corner, then working along 2nd side edge work 3 dc, 10 ch, skip 1 cm of the edge then work 4 dc in remainder of edge. Fasten off.

The yarn
is brought loosely up
the side edge.

Making up

Weave in all ends. Sew button to
middle of side edge to correspond
with button loop and to fit mug.

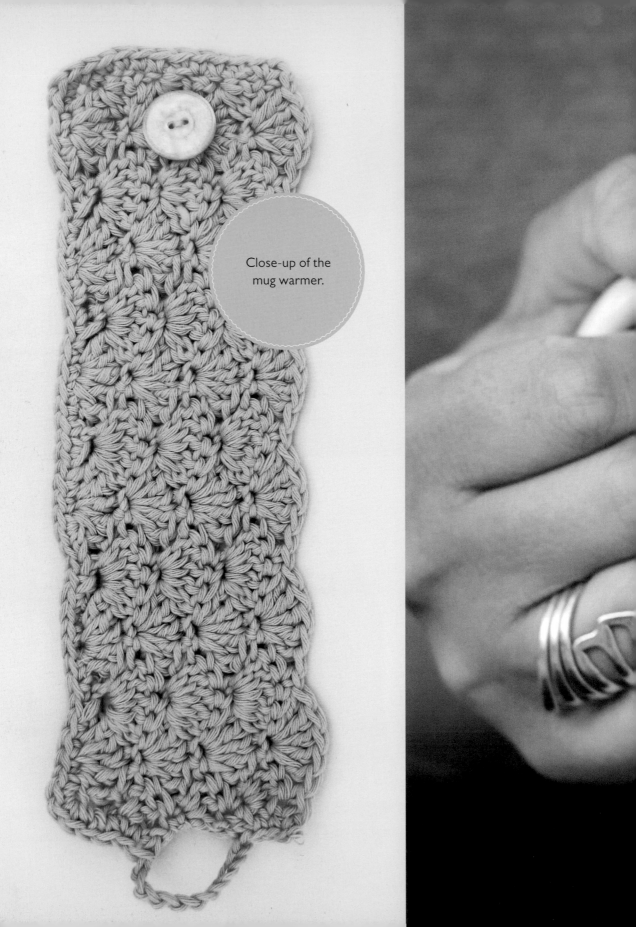

Close-up of the mug warmer.

Mug warmers keep your drinks warm and have a comforting feel.

BABY'S SWEATER

Eye-catching, cosy sweater for babies and toddlers: gorgeous for boys or girls.

Sizes

	3–6 months	12–18 months
To fit chest	46(18)	57.5(22½) cm (in)
Actual chest	51(20)	64(25) cm (in)
Back length	27(10½)	32(12½) cm (in)
Sleeve	17(6¾)	23(9) cm (in)

The instructions for the larger size are given in square brackets [ ] below. Where there are no brackets, the instructions apply to both sizes.

Materials

For the smaller sweater:

- MC – 2[3] x 50 g balls of Rowan Pure Wool shade Cypress 007

- A – 1[2] x 50 g balls of Rowan Pure Wool shade Pier 006

- B – 1[2] x 50 g balls of Rowan Pure Wool shade Enamel 013

For the larger sweater:

- MC – 2[3] x 50 g balls of Rowan Pure Wool shade Indigo 010

- A – 1[2] x 50 g balls of Rowan Pure Wool shade Parsley 020

- B – 1[2] x 50 g balls of Rowan Pure Wool shade Enamel 013

- 1 x 4 mm crochet hook (USG/6)

- 1 x 3.5 mm crochet hook (USE/4)

- 2 buttons

- wool sewing needle

To substitute yarn:
Use correct length of any DK yarn that has a standard knit tension of 22 sts and 28/30 rows to 10 cm square worked on 4 mm (US6) needles.

Abbreviations
beg = beginning
ch = chain
cont = continue
dc = double crochet
htr = half treble
rep = repeat
RS = right side
st = stitch
t-ch = turning chain
tr = treble
MC = main colour

Tension
Using a 4 mm hook and worked over colour pattern, 16 sts and 16 rows to 10 cm square. When you have worked the first few rows of the back the work should measure 25.5[32] cm (10[12½] in) across. In order for the sweater to be the size given, you will need to achieve this tension. If your work is too small, change to a larger hook and start again; if it is too large, change to a smaller hook and start again.

Note:
Do not cut yarns at the end of each row, but bring them loosely up the side edges as 'floats'.

The stitch pattern.

Use three shades of one colour or contrasting colours for your sweater.

The sweater looks good on baby boys or baby girls.

Make the sweater

Back

Using a 4 mm hook and MC, make a length of
43[53] ch and work as follows:

Row 1: 1 tr into 4th ch from hook (1st 3 ch
count as 1 tr) * 1 dc in next ch, 1 tr in
next ch, rep from * to last 1 ch, 1 tr in
last ch, drawing A through last 2 loops
(41[51] sts).

Row 2: With A, 3 t-ch (counts as 1 tr), * 1 dc in
next tr, 1 tr in next dc, rep from * to last
2 sts, 1 dc in next tr, 1 tr in 3rd of 3 t-ch,
drawing B through last 2 loops.

Row 3: With B, 3 t-ch (counts as 1 tr), * 1 tr in
next dc, 1 dc in next tr, rep from * to last
2 sts, 1 tr in next dc, 1 tr in 3rd of 3 t-ch,
drawing MC through last 2 loops.

Row 4: With MC, as row 2, drawing A through
last 2 loops.

Row 5: With A, as row 3, drawing B through last
2 loops.

Row 6: With B, as row 2, drawing MC through
last 2 loops.

Row 7: With MC, as row 3, drawing A through
last 2 loops.

Repeat rows 2–7 until 43[51] rows have been worked.
Work measures 27[32] cm. Fasten off.

Front

Work as given for the back until 25[29] rows have
been worked. Work measures 15.5[18] cm from beg.

Keep continuity of colour pattern and work as follows:

Divide for neck opening

Next row: 3 t-ch (counts as 1 tr), (1 dc in next tr,
1 tr in next dc) x 9[11], drawing next
colour through last 2 loops of last st
worked.

Turn and work as follows:

Next row: 3 t-ch (counts as 1 tr), (1 tr in next dc,
1 dc in next tr) x 8[10], 1 tr in next dc,
1 tr in 3rd of 3 t-ch, drawing next colour
through last 2 loops.

Next row: 3 t-ch (counts as 1 tr), (1 dc in next tr,
1 tr in next dc) x 8[10], 1 dc in next tr,
1 tr in 3rd of 3 t-ch, drawing next colour
through last 2 loops.

Rep these last two rows 3[4] more times, then rep
the 1st of these last two rows once more, ending at
armhole edge.

Shape neck

Next row: 3 t-ch (counts as 1 tr), (1 dc in next tr,
1 tr in next dc) x 8[10], 1 dc in next tr,
drawing next colour through last 2 loops.
Turn.

Next row: 1 ch (1 dc in next tr, 1 tr, in next dc) x
8[10], 1 tr in 3rd of 3 t-ch, drawing next
colour through last 2 loops. Turn.

Next row: 3 t-ch (counts as 1 tr), (1 dc in next tr,
1 tr in next dc) x 7[9], 1 dc in next tr,
drawing next colour through last 2 loops.
Turn.

Next row: 1 ch (1 dc in next tr, 1 tr, in next dc) x
7[9], 1 tr in 3rd of 3 t-ch, drawing next
colour through last 2 loops. Turn.

Next row: 3 t-ch (counts as 1 tr), (1 dc in next tr, 1 tr, in next dc) x 7[9], drawing next colour through last 2 loops. Turn.

Next row: 3 t-ch (counts as 1 tr), (1 tr in next dc, 1 dc in next tr) x 6[8], 1 tr in next dc, 1 tr in 3rd of 3 t-ch, drawing next colour through last 2 loops. Turn.

Next row: 3 t-ch (counts as 1 tr), (1 dc in next tr, 1 tr, in next dc) x 6[8], 1 dc in next tr, 1 tr in 3rd of 3 t-ch at beg of previous row, drawing next colour through last 2 loops. Turn.

The last two rows form the pattern, rep pattern 0[1] more times, rep the 1st of the last two rows once, ending with same pattern row as back. Fasten off.

Other side of neck

Count across 3[5] sts at centre front of neck and rejoin correct colour yarn with ss to next dc. Keep continuity of colour pattern and work as follows:

Next row: 3 t-ch (counts as 1 tr), (1 dc in next tr, 1 tr in next dc) x 8[10], 1 dc in next tr, 1 tr in 3rd of 3 t-ch, draw next colour through last 2 loops.

Next row: 3 t-ch (counts as 1 tr), (1 tr in next dc, 1 dc in next tr) x 8[10], 1 tr in next dc, 1 tr in 3rd of 3 t-ch, draw next colour through last 2 loops

Rep these last 2 rows 4[5] more times, ending at neck edge.

Shape neck

Next row: 1 ch, (1 dc in next tr, 1 tr in next dc) x 8[10], 1 dc in next tr, 1 tr in 3rd of 3 t-ch, draw next colour through last 2 loops. Turn.

Next row: 3 t-ch (counts as 1 tr), (1 tr in next dc, 1 dc in next tr) x 8[10], drawing next colour through last 2 loops. Turn.

Next row: 1 ch, (1 dc in next tr, 1 tr in next dc) x 7[9], 1 dc in next tr, 1 tr in 3rd of 3 t-ch, drawing next colour through last 2 loops. Turn.

Next row: 3 t-ch (counts as 1 tr), (1 tr in next dc, 1 dc in next tr) x 7[9], drawing next colour through last 2 loops. Turn.

Next row: 3 t-ch (counts as 1 tr), (1 dc in next tr, 1 tr in next dc) x 6[8], 1 dc in next tr, 1 tr in 3rd of 3 t-ch, drawing next colour through last 2 loops. Turn.

Next row: 3 t-ch (counts as 1 tr), (1 tr in next dc, 1 dc in next tr) x 6[8], 1 tr in next dc, 1 tr in 3rd of 3 t-ch, drawing next colour through last 2 loops. Turn.

The last two rows form the pattern, rep pattern 1[2] more times, ending with same pattern row as back. Fasten off.

Sleeves (make two)

Using a 3.5 mm hook and MC, make a length of 34[40] ch and work as follows:

Next row: 1 htr in 3rd ch from hook (1st 2 ch count as 1 htr), 1 htr in each ch to end of row (33[39] sts).

Next row: 2 t-ch (counts as 1 htr), skip 1st htr of row, 1 htr in each htr to end of row, working last htr in 2nd of 2 t-ch (35[41] htr).

Next row: 2 t-ch (counts as 1 htr), work 1 htr back into 1st htr of row, 1 htr in each htr to end of row, working last htr in 2nd of 2 t-ch, work another htr back into this same stitch (37[43] htr).

Now start to work colour pattern as given for the back until 10[12] rows of pattern have been worked. Change to a 4 mm hook and cont in pattern until work measures 17[23] cm (6¾[9¼] in). Fasten off.

Making up

Note: Make sure when sewing together that all the floats at the edge of work are brought to the wrong side of the work.

Pin out and press all the pieces according to ball-band instructions.

Place right sides of work together, pin the shoulders together and oversew them so that they lie flat when opened out.

TIP

When pressing, make sure you follow the instructions given for the yarn you are using. If you press an acrylic yarn using lots of heat or steam, the yarn will lose its body and the garment will become limp.

TIP

Work the buttonholes on the right-hand side for girls.

Right-hand side front band

With a 3.5 mm hook and MC, working from RS of the right-hand neck opening edge, join yarn with a ss to beginning of opening. Work 2 ch (counts as 1st htr) then work 15[17] htr evenly along the opening edge, making sure that any floats of yarn are enclosed within these stitches.

Next row: 2 t-ch (counts as 1 htr), skip 1st htr of row, then work 1 htr in each htr to end, working last htr in 2nd of 2 t-ch.

Rep this last row 1[2] more times. Fasten off.

Left-hand side front band

With a 3.5 mm hook and MC, and working from RS of the left-hand neck opening edge, join yarn with a ss to neck end of opening. Work 2 ch (counts as 1st htr), then work 15[17] htr evenly along the opening edge, making sure that any floats of yarn are enclosed within these stitches.

Next row (buttonhole row): 2 t-ch (counts as 1 htr), skip 1st htr of row, then work 1 htr in each of next 3[4] htr, 2 ch, skip 2 htr, 1 htr in each of next 5[6] htr, 2 ch, skip next 2 htr, 1 htr in each of next 2 htr, then work 1 htr in 2nd of 2 t-ch at end of row.

Next row: 2 t-ch (counts as 1 htr), skip 1st htr of row, then work 1 htr in each htr to end, working last htr in 2nd of 2 t-ch at end of row.

Rep last row 0[1] more time. Fasten off.

Collar

With a 3.5 mm hook and MC, working from RS of the neckline, rejoin yarn with ss to the centre of the right front band, work 2 ch (counts as 1st htr), then work 14[16] htr evenly round front neck to shoulder seam, work 22[24] htr along the back neck and 15[17] htr around the left front neck to centre of left front band (52[58] htr).

Next row: 2 t-ch (counts as 1 htr), skip 1st htr of row, then work 1 htr in each htr to end, working last htr in 2nd of 2 t-ch.

Repeat this last row 1[2] more times, then change to a 4 mm hook and work 3 more rows the same. Fasten off.

Fold top edge of sleeve in half and place this halfway point – with right sides together – at the shoulder seam.

Pin sleeves to body and oversew them so that they lie flat when opened out.

With right sides together, pin underarm seams of both sides from wrist to hem, oversew these so that they lie flat when opened out. Weave in all the ends.

Turn right side out and sew buttons in place to match buttonholes.

LACE PATTERNS:

LACE TABLE MAT

Learn to work simple lace patterns and make these pretty table mats at the same time.

Size
approx 16 cm (6¼ in) square

Materials
- 1 x 50 g ball each of Rico Creative Cotton Aran in shades 80 White, 64 Candy Pink and 16 Violet (85 m/95 yd per 50 g ball)

- 1 x 4.5 mm crochet hook (US nearest equivalent H/8)

To substitute yarn:
Use the correct length of any Aran weight yarn that has a standard knit tension of 18 sts and 24 rows to 10 cm square worked on 5 mm (US8) needles.

Tension
Although the tension and the size of the table mat are not important, if you want the table mat to be the size given, after the first few rows your work should measure 16 cm (6¼ in) wide. If your work is too small, change to a larger hook and start again; if it is too large, change to a smaller hook and start again.

Abbreviations
beg = beginning
ch = chain
cont = continue
dc = double crochet
htr = half treble
rep = repeat
st = stitch
t-ch = turning chain
tr = treble

For this pattern you will need a length of chain with a multiple of 2 sts + 3 sts.

Make the table mat

Using a 4.5 mm hook, make a length of 27 chain and work as follows:

Row 1:   1 tr in 4th ch from hook (1st 3 ch counts as 1 tr), 1 tr in each ch to end (25 tr).

Row 2:   3 t-ch (counts as 1 tr), 1 tr in 2nd tr of row, * skip 1 tr, (1 tr, 1 ch, 1 tr) all into next tr, rep from * to last 3 tr, skip 1 tr, 1 tr into next tr, 1 tr into 3rd of 3 t-ch.

Row 3:   3 t-ch (counts as first tr), 1 tr in 2nd tr of row, * (1 tr, 1 ch, 1 tr) into next 1 ch sp, rep from * to last 2 tr, 1 tr into next tr, 1 tr into 3rd of 3 t-ch.

Rep row 3, 10 more times in all.

Row 14:   3 t-ch (counts as first tr), 1 tr in 2nd tr of row, * 1 tr in next tr, skip next ch, 1 tr in next tr, rep from * to last 2 tr, 1 tr into next tr, 1 tr into 3rd of 3 t-ch.

Fasten off and weave in all ends.

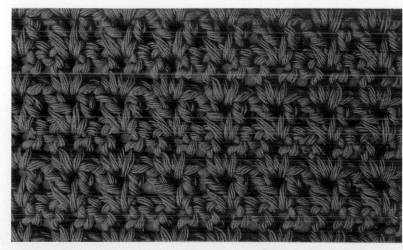

Close-up of the 'v' stitch pattern.

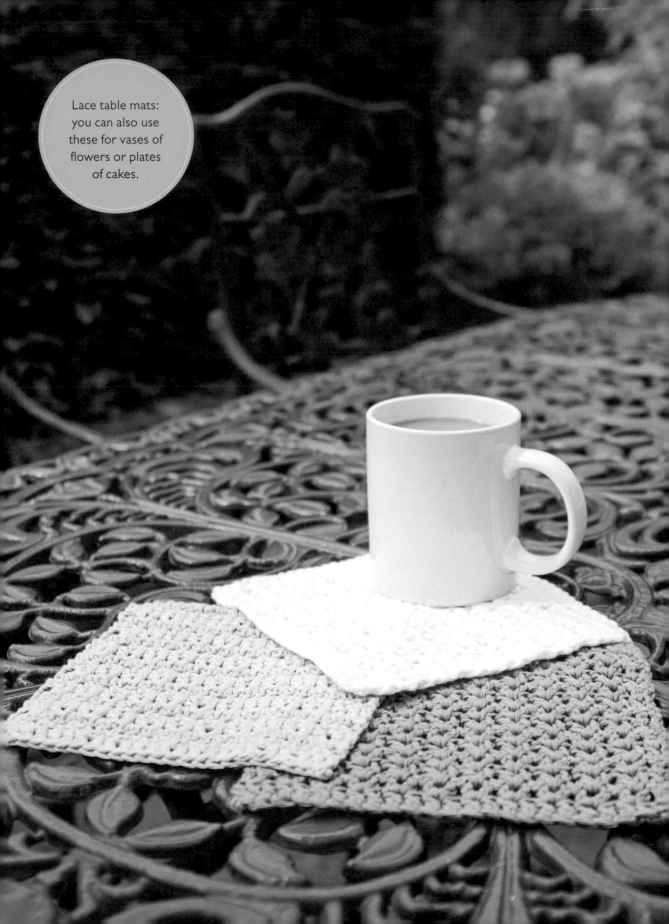

Lace table mats: you can also use these for vases of flowers or plates of cakes.

Close-up of
lace table mats.

SHELL LACE TABLE MAT

Size
approx 16 cm (6¼ in) square

Materials
- 1 x 50 g ball each of Rico Creative Cotton Aran in shades 80 White, 64 Candy Pink and 16 Violet (85 m/95 yd per 50 g ball)

- 1 x 4.5 mm crochet hook (US nearest equivalent H/8)

To substitute yarn:
Use the correct length of any Aran weight yarn that has a standard knit tension of 18 sts and 24 rows to 10 cm square worked on 5 mm (US8) needles.

Tension
Although the tension and the size of the table mat are not important, if you want the table mat to be the size given, when you have worked the first few rows the work should measure 16 cm (6¼ in) wide. If your work is too small, change to a larger hook and start again; if it is too large, change to a smaller hook and start again.

Abbreviations
ch = chain
dc = double crochet
rep = repeat
shell = work 5 tr into one stitch.
st = stitch
t-ch = turning chain
tr = treble

Simple shell stitch pattern

For this pattern you will need a length of chain with a multiple of 6 sts + 1 + stitches for the edge and turning ch.

Make the table mat

Using a 4.5 mm hook, make a length of 29 ch and work as follows:

Row 1:   1 tr in 4th ch from hook (1st 3 ch counts as 1 tr), 1 tr in each ch to end (27 tr).

Row 2:   3 t-ch (counts as 1 tr), 1 tr in each of next 2 tr of row, 3 ch, skip next 1 tr, * 1 dc in next tr, skip 2 tr, 1 shell into next tr, skip 2 tr, rep from * to last 5 tr, 1 dc in next tr, 3 ch, skip 1 tr, 1 tr in each of next 2 tr, 1 tr into 3rd of 3 t-ch.

Row 3:   1 t ch (does not count as first dc), 1 dc in each of 1st 3 tr, * 5 ch, 1 dc in centre tr of shell, rep from * ending 5 ch, 1 dc in each of next 2 tr, 1 dc in 3rd of 3 t-ch.

Row 4:   3 t-ch (counts as 1 tr), 1 tr in each of next 2 dc of row, * skip 2 ch, 1 shell into next ch, 1 dc in next dc, rep from * to last repeat skip 2 ch, 1 shell into next ch, 1 tr into each of last 3 dc.

Row 5:   1 t-ch (does not count as first dc), 1 dc in each of 1st 3 tr, 3 ch, 1 dc in centre tr of next shell, * 5 ch, 1 dc in centre tr of shell, rep from * ending 3 ch, 1 dc in each of next 2 tr of row, 1 dc into 3rd of 3 t-ch.

Row 6:   3 t-ch (counts as 1 tr), 1 tr in each of next 2 dc of row, 3 ch, * 1 dc in next dc, skip 2 ch, 1 shell into next ch, rep from * ending 1 dc in next dc, 3 ch, 1 tr into each of last 3 dc.

Repeat rows 3–6 once more, then rep rows 3, 4 and 5 once more.

Close-up of the shell stitch pattern.

Row 13:   3 t-ch (counts as first tr), 1 tr in each of next 2 dc of row, 2 tr in next 3 ch sp (working under the chain stitches – not into them), *1 tr in next dc, 4 tr in next 5 ch sp, rep from * ending 1 tr in next dc, 2 tr in next 3 ch sp, 1 tr in each of last 3 dc.

Fasten off and weave in ends.

LACE SHAWL

This light and airy shawl uses the basic stitches that you have already practised.

Size
53 cm (20¾ in) x 190 cm (75¾ in)

Materials
- 3 x 50 g balls of Debbie Bliss Rialto Lace (390 m per ball)

- 1 x 4 mm hook

To substitute yarn:
Use correct length of any laceweight yarn, working to the tension given below, or use correct length of any 4 ply yarn that has a standard knit tension of 28 sts and 36 rows to 10 cm square worked on 3.25 mm (US3) needles.

Tension
1 pattern repeat measures 5 cm (2 in) square

Abbreviations
ch = chain
dc = double crochet
dtr = double treble
picot = work 3 ch, then work 1 dc back into the 1st of these 3 ch
rep = repeat
RS = right side
sp = space
st = stitch
t-ch = turning chain
tr = treble

The shawl.

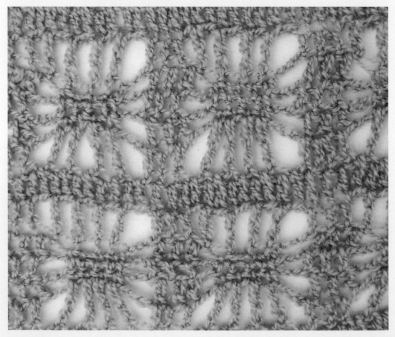

Close-up of shawl worked in laceweight yarn.

Make the shawl

Note: this pattern is worked using very fine yarn with a 4 mm hook. It is important to work the stitches loosely so that the work is light and lacy. Check your tension.

You will need a length of chain with a multiple of 12 stitches + edge stitches and turning chain.

Using a 4 mm hook, make a length of 131 ch and work as follows.

Row 1: 1 tr into 4th ch from hook (1st 3 ch counts as 1 tr), 1 tr into every ch to end (129 tr).

Row 2: 3 t-ch (counts as 1 tr), skip 1st tr, then work 1 tr in each tr to end of row, (working last tr in 3rd of 3 t-ch – do this throughout pattern) (129 tr).

Row 3: 3 t-ch (counts as 1 tr), skip 1st tr, 1 tr into each of next 5 tr, * 3 ch, (skip next tr, 1 dtr into next tr) x 4, skip next tr, 3 ch, 1 tr into each of next 3 tr, rep from * to last 3 tr, 1 tr in each of last 3 tr.

Work should measure 53 cm (20¾ in) across and there are 10 repeats.

Row 4: 3 t-ch (counts as 1 tr), skip 1st tr, 1 tr into each of next 5 tr, * 3 ch, 1 dc into each of next 4 dtr, 3 ch, 1 tr into each of next 3 tr, rep from * to to last 3 tr, 1 tr in each of last 3 tr.

Row 5: 3 t-ch (counts as 1 tr), skip 1st tr, 1 tr into each of next 5 tr, * 3 ch, 1 dc into each of next 4 dc, 3 ch, 1 tr into each of next 3 tr, rep from * to to last 3 tr, 1 tr in each of last 3 tr.

Row 6: Work the same as row 5.

Row 7: 3 t-ch (counts as 1 tr), skip 1st tr, 1 tr into each of next 5 tr, * (1 ch, 1 dtr into next dc) x 4, 1 ch, 1 tr into each of next 3 tr, rep from * to last 3 tr, 1 tr in each of last 3 tr.

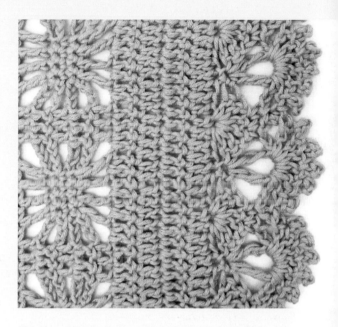

Close-up of shawl pattern worked in a standard 4 ply yarn.

Row 8: 3 t-ch (counts as 1 tr), skip 1st tr, 1 tr into each of next 5 tr, * (1 tr in next ch, 1 tr in next dtr) x 4, 1 tr in next ch, 1 tr in each of next 3 tr, rep from * to last 3 tr, 1 tr in each of last 3 tr (129 tr).

TIP

Count the trebles at the end of the eighth row and before starting a new pattern repeat. This way you will maintain the correct number of stitches throughout the work.

Rows 3–8 form the pattern – repeat these 6 rows until 36 pattern repeats have been worked, ending with an eighth pattern row. Now work row 2 once more (129 sts). Fasten off. Place marker to mark right side of work.

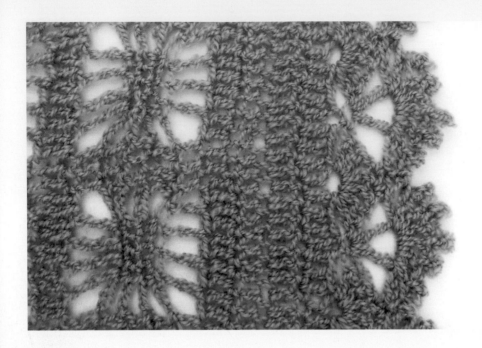

The border is worked after the main part has been completed.

Border

With RS of work facing and using a 4 mm hook, rejoin yarn to foundation chain at right-hand corner by working a slip stitch into the first ch, then work as follows:

Row 1: (RS) 3 ch (counts as 1st tr), 1 tr into next st, 1 tr into each st to end (129 tr).

Row 2: 3 t-ch (counts as 1 st tr), skip 1st tr of row, * 1 tr into next tr rep from * to end – working last tr into 3rd of 3 t-ch at end of row (129 tr).

Row 3: (RS) 3 t-ch (counts as 1st tr), (1 tr, 1 ch, 2 tr), all worked into 1st tr of row, * skip next 3 tr, 1 dc in next tr, skip next 3 tr, (2 tr, 1 ch, 2 tr, 1 ch, 2 tr) all worked into next tr, repeat from * to last 8 tr, skip next 3 tr, 1 dc in next tr, (2 tr, 1 ch, 2 tr) all worked into 3rd of 3 t-ch at end of row.

Row 4: 1 t-ch, 1 dc in each of 1st 2 tr, * 2 ch, (1 dtr, 1 ch, 1 dtr) all worked into next dc, skip next 2 tr and 1 ch, 2 ch, 1 dc in next tr, 1 picot, 1 dc in next tr, rep from * to last rep, 2 ch, (1 dtr, 1 ch, 1 dtr) all worked into next dc, 2 ch, 1 dc in each of last 2 tr.

Row 5: (RS) 2 ch, * ([1 tr, 1 picot] x 5, 1 tr), all worked into next 1 ch sp, 1 dc in next picot, rep from * to end, working last dc into last dc of row. Fasten off.

With RS facing, rejoin yarn to other end and working into the last row of trebles work the border as given above.

Making up

Pin out and press according to ball-band instructions. Sew in all ends.

TIP

For large projects like this you can place a clean towel on the carpet and pin your work to it to stretch it out when finished.

This shawl makes a lovely light cover-up for summer evenings.

8

Squares and circles

The granny square blanket is perhaps the most iconic of all crochet projects. These amazing and colourful blankets are made from individual squares or motifs. Motifs can be made in all sorts of shapes and sizes: squares, triangles, circles, hexagons and more. They can then be joined together to make a variety of projects such as blankets, shawls, bags, slippers, scarves etc. In this chapter we will be learning how to make the granny square and the granny circle.

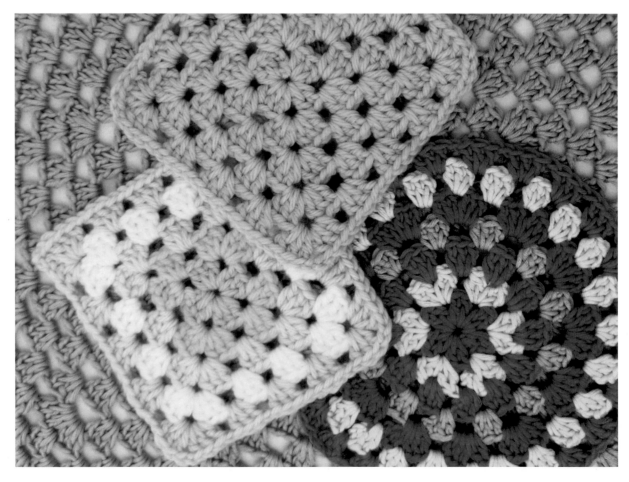

A selection of squares and circles.

SQUARES

The most iconic image of crochet is the granny square. Not just for grannies any more though, granny squares have become hot fashion items. They have been seen on catwalks and have even been translated into printed items for bed linen, carpets, T-shirts, shoes and tights.

Working the granny square is easy now that you have mastered all the basic stitches.

The basic granny square consists of working in rounds from one central circle of chain. Increases are made at the corners so that the work becomes a square as it grows. A square can be increased until it becomes one big square, or small squares can be made and then joined together.

This beautiful lined bag shows the versatility of crochet granny squares. Crochet bag design by Ingunn Santini. The pattern includes a tutorial for the lining with pocket, and is available in the Etsy shop Sophie and Me at www.etsy.com/shop/PdfPatternDesign.

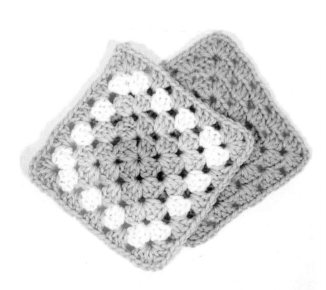

The basic granny square.

Increases are made at the corner of each square.

GRANNY SQUARE, ONE-COLOUR AND MULTICOLOURED

Size
approx 11 cm (4½ in) square when worked on a 4 mm hook with DK yarn

Materials

For the one-colour version:

- 1 x 50 g ball of Artesano Superwash Merino in shade Baby Lavender 5769 (112 m/122 yd per 50 g ball)

For the multicoloured version:

- 1 x 50 g ball each of Artesano Superwash Merino in shades Baby Lavender 5769, Baby Pink 0043, Baby Green 8361, White 0157, Baby Teal 5771

- 1 x 4 mm crochet hook (USG/6)

To substitute yarn:
Use any DK yarn that has a standard knit tension of 22 sts and 28/30 rows to 10 cm square worked on 4 mm (US6) needles.

Tension
Tension is not important.

Abbreviations
beg = beginning
ch = chain
dc = double crochet
rep = repeat
sp = space
ss = slip stitch
tr = treble

The basic granny square.

Make the one-coloured square

Using a 4 mm hook, make a length of 4 ch and join into a ring by working ss into the 1st of these ch.

Round 1: 3 ch (counts as 1 tr), 2 tr into ring, * 2 ch, 3 tr into ring, rep from * 2 more times, 1 ch, 1 dc into 3rd of 3 ch at beg of round.

Round 2: 3 ch (counts as 1 tr), 2 tr into dc sp, * 1 ch, (3 tr, 2 ch, 3 tr) all worked into next 2 ch sp, rep from * 2 more times, 1 ch, 3 tr back into 1st sp, 1 ch, 1 dc into 3rd of 3 ch at beg of round.

Round 3: 3 ch (counts as 1 tr), 2 tr into dc sp, * 1 ch, 3 tr in next 1 ch sp, 1 ch, (3 tr, 2 ch, 3 tr) all worked into next 2 ch sp, rep from * 2 more times, 1 ch, 3 tr in next 1 ch sp, 1 ch, 3 tr back into 1st sp, 1 ch, 1 dc into 3rd of 3 ch at beg of round.

Round 4: 3 ch (counts as 1 tr), 2 tr into dc sp, * (1 ch, 3 tr in next 1 ch sp) x 2, 1 ch, (3 tr, 2 ch, 3 tr) all worked into next 2 ch sp, rep from * 2 more times, (1 ch , 3 tr in next 1 ch sp) x 2, 1 ch, 3 tr back into 1st sp, 1 ch, 1 dc into 3rd of 3 ch at beg of round.

Round 5: 3 ch (counts as 1 tr), 2 tr into dc sp, * (1 ch, 3 tr in next 1 ch sp) x 3, 1 ch, (3 tr, 2 ch, 3 tr) all worked into next 2 ch sp, rep from * 2 more times, (1 ch , 3 tr in next 1 ch sp) x 3, 1 ch, 3 tr back into 1st sp, 1 ch, 1 dc into 3rd of 3 ch at beg of round.

For larger squares, continue working round 5, **and** increase – by one – the number of times the underlined instructions are worked for each extra round. Weave in ends when finished.

Make the multicoloured square

Note: Cut the yarn not being used and weave in the ends when work is finished.

Using a 4 mm hook, make a length of 4 ch and join into a ring by working ss into the 1st of these ch.

Round 1: 3 ch (counts as 1 tr), 2 tr into ring, * 2 ch, 3 tr into ring, rep from * 2 more times, 1 ch, 1 dc into 3rd of 3 ch at beg of round, drawing the new colour through last 2 loops worked.

Round 2: Using new colour, 3 ch (counts as 1 tr), 2 tr into dc sp, * 1 ch, (3 tr, 2 ch, 3 tr) all worked into next 2 ch sp, rep from * 2 more times, 1 ch, 3 tr back into 1st sp, 1 ch, 1 dc into 3rd of 3 ch at beg of round, drawing the new colour through last 2 loops worked.

Round 3:   Using new colour, 3 ch (counts as 1 tr), 2 tr into dc sp, * 1 ch, 3 tr in next 1 ch sp, 1 ch, (3 tr, 2 ch, 3 tr) all worked into next 2 ch sp, rep from * 2 more times, 1 ch , 3 tr in next 1 ch sp, 1 ch, 3 tr back into 1st sp, 1 ch, 1 dc into 3rd of 3 ch at beg of round, drawing the new colour through last 2 loops worked.

Round 4:   Using new colour, 3 ch (counts as 1 tr), 2 tr into dc sp, * (1 ch, 3 tr in next 1 ch sp) x 2, 1 ch, (3 tr, 2 ch, 3 tr) all worked into next 2 ch sp, rep from * 2 more times, (1 ch, 3 tr in next 1 ch sp) x 2, 1 ch, 3 tr back into 1st sp, 1 ch, 1 dc into 3rd of 3 ch at beg of round, drawing the new colour through last 2 loops worked.

Round 5:   Using new colour, 3 ch (counts as 1 tr), 2 tr into dc sp, * <u>(1 ch, 3 tr in next 1 ch sp) x 3,</u> 1 ch, (3 tr, 2 ch, 3 tr) all worked into next 2 ch sp, rep from * 2 more times, <u>(1 ch, 3 tr in next 1 ch sp) x 3,</u> 1 ch, 3 tr back into 1st sp, 1 ch, 1 dc into 3rd of 3 ch at beg of round, drawing the new colour through last 2 loops worked.

For larger squares, continue working round 5, **and** increase – by one – the number of times the <u>underlined instructions</u> are worked for each extra round **and** changing the colour as required.

Weave in all the ends when finished.

The basic multicoloured granny square.

Sewing the granny squares together

The squares can be joined in a number of different ways. Here I show you how to join them by sewing the squares together.

Working from the wrong side, or with right sides placed together, oversew or whip the edges together, taking care to match the chain stitches and working into each chain stitch of each square. The sample shown here uses contrast yarn, but you would normally use matching yarn so that the stitches don't show.

GRANNY-SQUARE PRAM BLANKET

Your first granny-square project is so pretty: a great gift for a new baby.

Size
58 cm (22¾ in) x 48 cm (19 in)

Materials
- 2 x 50 g balls each of Artesano Superwash Merino DK in White 0157 and Baby Green 8361

- 1 x 50 g balls each of Artesano Superwash Merino DK in Baby Pink 0043 and Baby Teal 5771

- 1 x 4 mm crochet hook (USG/6)

To substitute yarn:
Use any DK yarn that has a standard knit tension of 22 sts and 28/30 rows to 10 cm square worked on 4 mm (US6) needles.

Tension
Tension is not important, but to achieve the measurements given each 4-row square should measure 9 cm (3½ in) square when worked on a 4 mm hook with DK yarn. If your work is too small, change to a larger hook and start again; if it is too large, change to a smaller hook and start again.

Abbreviations
beg = beginning
ch = chain
dc = double crochet
rep = repeat
sp = space
ss = slip stitch
tr = treble

Note:
Cut yarns each time you change colour. This will leave you with a lot of ends to weave in, which you can do as you finish each square or when the blanket is complete. Sewing in the ends can be rather boring – a good time to watch *Mamma Mia* again!

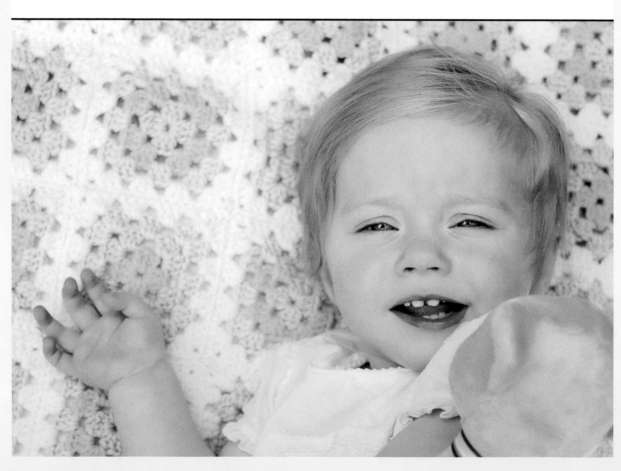

The blanket.

Make the blanket

Colourway 1 (make 15 squares)

Using a 4 mm hook and teal yarn, make a length of 4 ch and join with ss to 1st of these ch, to make a ring.

Round 1: With teal yarn, 3 ch (counts as 1 tr), 2 tr into ring, * 2 ch, 3 tr into ring, rep from * 2 more times, 1 ch, 1 dc into 3rd of 3 ch at beg of round   pull pink yarn through last 2 loops worked.

Round 2: With pink yarn, 3 ch (counts as 1 tr), 2 tr into dc sp, * 1 ch, (3 tr, 2 ch, 3 tr) all worked into next 2 ch sp, rep from * 2 more times, 1 ch, 3 tr back into 1st sp, 1 ch, 1 dc into 3rd of 3 ch at beg of round – pull green yarn through last 2 loops worked.

Round 3: With green yarn, 3 ch (counts as 1 tr), 2 tr into dc sp, * 1 ch, 3 tr in next 1 ch sp, 1 ch, (3 tr, 2 ch, 3 tr) all worked into next 2 ch sp, rep from * 2 more times, 1 ch, 3 tr in next 1 ch sp, 1 ch, 3 tr back into 1st sp, 1 ch, 1 dc into 3rd of 3 ch at beg of round – pull white yarn through last 2 loops worked.

Round 4: With white yarn, 3 ch (counts as 1 tr), 2 tr into dc sp, * (1 ch, 3 tr in next 1 ch sp) x 2, 1 ch, (3 tr, 2 ch, 3 tr) all worked into next 2 ch sp, rep from * 2 more times, (1 ch, 3 tr in next 1 ch sp) x 2, 1 ch, 3 tr back into 1st sp, 1 ch, 1 dc into 3rd of 3 ch at beg of round. Fasten off.

Colourway 2 (make 15 squares)

Work as for colourway 1, but working the colours as follows: round 1 = pink, round 2 = teal, rounds 3 and 4 the same as colourway 1.

Joining

Weave in all the ends.

Arrange the squares in a chequerboard design (alternating the two colourways) five squares by six squares. Working from the wrong side of the work, oversew the squares together, matching the stitches so that the sewing is even and lies flat.

The shell border.

Using a 4 mm hook and cream yarn, and with RS facing, join to work with a ss worked into the corner chain space at right-hand end of a short edge.

Round 1: 1 ch (counts as 1 dc) * (4 ch, 1 dc in next 1 ch sp) x 3, 4 ch, dc in join between squares *, rep from * to * 3 more times, (4 ch, 1 dc in next 1 ch sp) x 3, 4 ch, 1 dc in 2 ch sp at corner, 4 ch, 1 dc back into 2 ch sp at corner, now rep from * to * 5 times along long edge, (4 ch, 1 dc in next 1 ch sp) x 3, 4 ch, 1 dc in 2 ch sp at corner, 4 ch, 1 dc back into 2 ch sp at corner, now rep from * to * 4 times along short edge, (4 ch, 1 dc in next 1 ch sp) x 3, 4 ch, 1 dc in next 2 ch sp at corner, 4 ch, 1 dc back into 2 ch sp at corner, now rep from * to * 5 times along next long edge, (4 ch, 1 dc in next 1 ch sp) x 3, 4 ch, 1 dc in next 2 ch sp at corner, 1 ch, 1 tr into 1st ss.

Round 2: 3 ch (counts as 1 tr), 2 tr back into same treble sp, * ss into next dc, 5 tr into next 4 ch sp, rep from * all round blanket and end with ss into next dc, 2 tr into last treble sp, ss to 3rd of 3 ch at beg of round.

Fasten off and weave in any remaining ends.

GRANNY SQUARE SLIPPERS FOR MEN

These slippers are bright, stylish, warm and easy to make: a perfect stocking-filler.

Size
26 cm (10¼ in) – to fit a UK shoe size from 7 to 11

Materials
- 1 x 100 g ball of Noro Silk Garden sock yarn 008 (300 m/334 yd per 50 g ball)

- 1 x 4 mm crochet hook (USG/6)

To substitute yarn:
Use correct length of any DK weight yarn that has a standard knit tension of 22 sts and 28 rows to 10 cm square worked on 4 mm (US6) needles.

Tension
If you want the slippers to be the size given, a completed square should measure approx 10 cm (4 in) square. If your work is too small, change to a larger hook and start again; if it is too large, change to a smaller hook and start again.

Abbreviations
beg = beginning
ch = chain
dc = double crochet
rep = repeat
sp = space
ss = slip stitch
t-ch = turning chain
tr = treble

TIP

When making slippers or socks, always use a yarn that contains a small percentage of nylon. This will help them to last longer.

These comfy slippers will keep your feet warm and cosy.

The pair of slippers use 12 solid squares like this.

Make the slippers (work 6 squares for each slipper)

With a 4 mm hook, make a length of 4 ch and join into a ring by working a ss into 1st of these ch.

Round 1: 3 t ch (counts as 1 tr), 2 tr into ring, * 2 ch, 3 tr, into ring, rep from * twice more, 1 ch, 1 dc into 3rd of 3 t-ch at beg of round.

Round 2: 3 t-ch (counts as 1 tr), 1 tr into the dc sp, * 1 tr into each of next 3 tr, 2 tr into next 2 ch sp, 2 ch, 2 tr into same 2 ch sp, rep from * twice more, 1 tr into each of next 3 tr, 2 tr into last ch sp, 1 ch, 1 dc into 3rd of 3 t-ch at beg of round.

Round 3: 3 t-ch (counts as 1 tr), 1 tr into the dc sp, * 1 tr into each of next 7 tr, 2 tr into next 2 ch sp, 2 ch, 2 tr into same 2 ch sp, rep from * twice more, 1 tr into each of next 7 tr, 2 tr into last ch sp, 1 ch, 1 dc into 3rd of 3 t-ch at beg of round.

Round 4: 3 t-ch (counts as 1 tr), 1 tr into the dc sp, * 1 tr into each of next 11 tr, 2 tr into next 2 ch sp, 2 ch, 2 tr into same 2 ch sp, rep from * twice more, 1 tr into each of next 11 tr, 2 tr into last ch sp, 1 ch, 1 dc into 3rd of 3 t-ch at beg of round.

TIP

When working in *rounds* from the right side only, the hook is inserted to the right of each stitch – when working in *rows* you are working into the wrong side of the work and the hook is inserted to the left of each stitch.

Triangle (work 2 for each slipper)

Note: work the edge stitches loosely.

With a 4 mm hook, make a length of 4 ch and join into a ring by working a ss into 1st of these ch.

Round 1: 3 t-ch (counts as 1 tr), 2 tr into ring, 2 ch, 3 tr into ring. Turn.

Round 2: 3 t-ch (counts as 1 tr), 2 tr back into 1st tr of row, 1 tr into each of next 2 tr, 2 tr into next 2 ch sp, 2 ch, 2 tr into same 2 ch sp, 1 tr into each of next 2 tr, 3 tr into to 3rd of 3 t-ch.

Round 3: 3 t-ch (counts as 1 tr), 2 tr back into 1st tr of row, 1 tr into each of next 6 tr, 2 tr into next 2 ch sp, 2 ch, 2 tr into same 2 ch sp, 1 tr into each of next 6 tr, 3 tr into to 3rd of 3 t-ch.

Round 4: 3 t-ch (counts as 1 tr), 2 tr back into 1st tr of row, 1 tr into each of next 10 tr, 2 tr into next 2 ch sp, 2 ch, 2 tr into same 2 ch sp, 1 tr into each of next 10 tr, 3 tr into to 3rd of 3 t-ch.

Making up

Working from the inside of the slipper, oversew the squares together using the diagram as a guide.

Cuff

With a 4 mm hook and with RS facing, rejoin yarn with ss to centre back of work at heel.

Round 1: 3 t-ch (counts as 1 tr), work 25 tr to centre front point, work 1 tr in centre front point, then work 25 tr along 2nd edge to beginning of round, ss to 3rd of 3 t-ch (52 tr).

Round 2: 3 t-ch (counts as 1 tr), skip 1st tr of round, work 1 tr in each tr to end of round, ss to 3rd of 3 t-ch (52 tr).

Rep round 2 until 5 rounds have been worked in all. Fasten off and weave in ends.

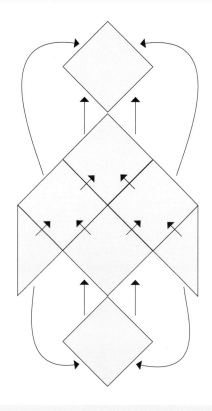

Place the triangles in position as shown, joining seams as shown by the arrows, and oversew them together. Weave in all ends and turn right side out.

CIRCLES

Circles are worked in a similar way to squares, but the increases are worked evenly around the work rather than at the corners. The gap between increases in each round increases as the circle gets bigger.

A granny circle worked using several colours.

BASIC GRANNY CIRCLE

Size
42 cm (16½ in) diameter after 19 rounds

Materials

For the one-coloured granny circle:

- 2 x 50 g balls of Rico Essentials Cotton DK shade 95 Aqua (130 m/143 yd per 50 g ball)

- 1 x 4 mm crochet hook (USG/6)

For the multicoloured granny circle:

- A – 1 x 50 g balls of Rico Essentials Cotton DK shade 70 Melon (130 m per ball)

- B – 1 x 50 g balls of Rico Essentials Cotton DK shade 86 Pistachio (130 m per ball)

- C – 1 x 50 g balls of Rico Essentials Cotton DK shade 14 Fuchsia (130 m per ball)

- D – 1 x 50 g balls of Rico Essentials Cotton DK shade 95 Aqua (130 m per ball)

To substitute yarn:
Use correct length of any DK yarn that has a standard knit tension of 22 sts and 28/30 rows to 10 cm square worked on 4 mm (US6) needles.

Tension
The tension is not important, but after three rounds the diameter should measure 8 cm.

Abbreviations
beg = beginning
ch = chain
dc = double crochet
rep = repeat
sp = space
ss = slip stitch
t-ch = turning chain
tr = treble
yoh = yarn over hook
2 tr bobble = yoh, insert hook into st, yoh, draw through, yoh, draw through 2 loops, rep from * once more – working into the same st, yoh, draw through all 3 loops on the hook

The granny circle can be made any size to use as a coaster or a blanket.

Make the granny circle

Using a 4 mm hook, make a length of 4 ch and join into a ring by working ss into the first of these ch.

Round 1: Work into the circle as follows: 3 t-ch (counts as 1 tr), 1 tr, * 1 ch, 2 tr * rep from * 4 more times, join with 1 dc into 3rd of 3 t-ch at beg of round. (There are 6 x 1 ch sp – counting the last 1 dc sp as one of these – and throughout work.)

Round 2: 3 t-ch (counts as 1 tr), (1 tr, 1 ch, 2 tr bobble) all worked into the 1 dc space, * 1 ch, (2 tr bobble, 1 ch, 2 tr bobble) all worked into next 1 ch sp. * rep from * 4 more times, join with 1 dc into 3rd of 3 t-ch at beg of round (12 x 1 ch sp).

Round 3: 3 t-ch (counts as 1 tr), 2 tr worked into the 1 dc space, *1 ch, 3 tr worked into next sp, rep from * to end of round, 1 dc into 3rd of 3 t-ch at beg of round (12 x 1 ch sp).

Round 4: As round 3.

Round 5: 3 t-ch (counts as 1 tr), (2 tr, 1 ch, 3 tr) all worked into the 1 dc space, * (1 ch, 3 tr) x 2 worked into next sp, rep from * to end of round, 1 dc into 3rd of 3 t-ch at beg of round (24 x 1 ch sp).

Rounds 6 and 7: As round 3.

Round 8: 3 t-ch (counts as 1 tr), (2 tr, 1 ch, 3 tr) all worked into the 1 dc space, * 1 ch, 3 tr into next ch sp, (1 ch, 3 tr) x 2 worked into next sp, rep from * to end of round 1 dc into 3rd of 3 t ch at beg of round. (36 x 1 ch sp).

Round 9, 10 and 11: As round 3.

Round 12: 3 t-ch (counts as 1 tr), (2 tr, 1 ch, 3 tr) all worked into the 1 dc sp, * (1 ch, 3 tr into next ch sp) x 2, (1 ch, 3 tr) x 2 worked into next sp, rep from * to end of round, 1 dc into 3rd of 3 t-ch at beg of round (18 x 1 ch sp).

Round 13, 14 and 15: As round 3.

Round 16: 3 t-ch (counts as 1 tr), (2 tr, 1 ch, 3 tr) all worked into the 1 dc space, * (1 ch, 3 tr into next ch sp) x 3, (1 ch, 3 tr) x 2 worked into next sp, rep from * to end of round, 1 dc into 3rd of 3 t-ch at beg of round (60 ch sp).

Round 17, 18 and 19: As round 3.

To make the circle larger, continue in the same manner: starting with an increase round (as given for round 16), and on each increase round, increase – by one – the number of times that the underlined instructions are worked, work three rounds of round 3 between each increase round.

Make a multicoloured granny circle

With colour A and a 4 mm hook, make a length of 4 ch and join into a circle by working a ss into 1st of these ch.

Round 1: Work into the circle as follows: 3 t-ch (counts as 1 tr) 1 tr, * 1 ch, 2 tr * repeat from * 4 more times, join with 1 dc into 3rd of 3 t-ch at beg of round – drawing colour B through last 2 loops. (There are 6 x 1 ch sp – counting the last 1 dc sp as one of these – and throughout work.)

Round 2: 3 t-ch (counts as 1 tr), (1 tr, 1 ch, 2 tr bobble) all worked into the 1 dc space, * 1 ch, (2 tr bobble, 1 ch, 2 tr bobble) all worked into next 1 ch sp, * repeat from * 4 more times, join with 1 dc into 3rd of 3 t-ch at beg of round – drawing colour C through last 2 loops (12 x 1 ch sp).

Round 3: 3 t-ch (counts as 1 tr), 2 tr worked into the 1 dc space, *1 ch, 3 tr worked into next sp, rep from * to end of round, 1 dc into 3rd of 3 t-ch at beg of round – drawing colour D through last 2 loops (12 x 1 ch sp).

Round 4: With colour D, as round 3 and drawing colour A through last 2 loops worked.

To make the circle larger, continue as for the one-colour circle, alternating colours in sequence as given here.

The multicoloured granny circle.

Making projects using circles

Crocheted circles are very versatile and can be incorporated in a number of items. Here are a few ways to use them.

BABY HAT

A pretty hat for a little girl. This project uses a circle for the top of the hat but continues without increases to form the tube part of the hat. The flowers are also made from circles and can be used on their own as bag charms or brooches.

Size
45 cm (17¾ in) circumference (the hat has some stretch) x 18 cm (7 in) deep – to fit a child aged around 12 months

Materials
- 1 x 50 g ball each of Sirdar Snuggly Baby Bamboo DK in shades Rinky Dinky Pink 158 and Babe 134 (95 m/104 yd per 50 g ball)

- 1 x 4 mm crochet hook (USG/6)

- 1 x 6 mm crochet hook (USJ/10)

- 2 buttons, 1 small and 1 large

- wool sewing needle

To substitute yarn:
Use correct length of any DK yarn that has a standard knit tension of 22 sts and 28/30 rows to 10 cm square worked on 4 mm (US6) needles.

Tension
After the first four rounds the diameter should measure 10 cm (4 in). In order for the hat to be the size given you will need to achieve this tension. If your work is too small, change to a larger hook and start again; if it is too large, change to a smaller hook and start again.

Abbreviations
beg = beginning
ch = chain
dc = double crochet
rep = repeat
sp = space
ss = slip stitch
t-ch – turning chain
tr = treble
yoh = yarn over hook
2 tr bobble = yoh, insert hook into st, yoh, draw through, yoh, draw through 2 loops, rep from * once more – working into the same st, yoh, draw through all 3 loops on the hook

3 tr bobble = yoh, insert hook into st, yoh, draw through, yoh, draw through 2 loops, rep from * twice more – working into the same st, yoh, draw through all 4 loops on the hook

The baby hat.

Make the hat

Using a 4 mm hook, make a length of 4 ch and join into a ring by working ss into the first of these ch.

Round 1: Working into the ring, work: 3 t-ch, 2 tr bobble, * 2 ch, 3 tr bobble, rep from * 3 more times, 1 tr in 3rd of 3 t-ch at beg of round (5 bobbles counting 1st 3 t-ch + 2 tr bobble as 1 bobble).

Round 2: 3 t-ch, 2 tr bobble into first 1 tr sp, 2 ch, 3 tr bobble back into same 1 tr sp, * (2 ch, 3 tr bobble) x 2 worked into next 2 ch sp, rep from * 3 more times, 1 tr in 3rd of 3 t-ch at beg of round (10 bobbles counting 1st 3 t-ch + 2 tr bobble as 1 bobble).

Round 3: 3 t-ch, 2 tr bobble into first 1 tr sp, * (2 ch, 3 tr bobble) x 2 worked into next 2 ch sp, 2 ch, 3 tr bobble worked into next 2 ch sp, rep from * 3 more times, (2 ch, 3 tr bobble) x 2 worked into last 2 ch sp, 1 tr in 3rd of 3 t-ch at beg of round (15 bobbles counting 1st 3 t-ch + 2 tr bobble as 1 bobble).

Round 4: 3 t-ch, 2 tr bobble into first 1 tr sp, * (2 ch, 3 tr bobble) x 2 worked into next 2 ch sp, (2 ch, 3 tr bobble worked into next 2 ch sp) x 2, rep from * 3 more times, (2 ch, 3 tr bobble) x 2 worked into next 2 ch sp, 2 ch, 3 tr bobble into next 2 ch sp, 1 tr in 3rd of 3 t-ch at beg of round (20 bobbles counting 1st 3 t-ch + 2 tr bobble as 1 bobble).

At this point work should measure 10 cm (4 in) diameter.

Round 5: 3 t-ch, 2 tr bobble into first 1 tr sp, * (2 ch, 3 tr bobble) x 2 worked into next 2 ch sp, (2 ch, 3 tr bobble worked into next 2 ch sp) x 4, rep from * 3 more times, (2 ch, 3 tr bobble) x 2 worked into next 2 ch sp, (2 ch, 3 tr bobble worked into next 2 ch sp) x 3, 1 tr in 3rd of 3 t-ch at beg of round (24 bobbles counting 1st 3 t-ch + 2 tr bobble as 1 bobble).

Round 6: 3 t-ch, 2 tr bobble into first 1 tr sp, * 2 ch, 3 tr bobble worked into next 2 ch sp, rep from * to end of round, 1 tr in 3rd of 3 t-ch at beg of round (24 bobbles counting 1st 3 t-ch + 2 tr bobble as 1 bobble).

Repeat round 6, five more times.

Round 12: 3 t-ch, 2 tr bobble into first 1 tr sp, * 2 ch, 3 tr bobble worked into next 2 ch sp, rep from * to end of round, 1 ch, 1 dc in 3rd of 3 t-ch at beg of round, drawing the pale pink through last 2 loops of last tr (cut the dark pink leaving ends to weave in later) (24 bobbles counting 1st 3 ch + 2 tr bobble as 1 bobble).

Continue in pale pink as follows:

Shell border

Round 1: With pale pink and a 4 mm hook, 1 t-ch, (counts as dc), * 5 tr in next 2 ch sp, 1 dc in next 2 ch sp, rep from * to last repeat, 5 tr in next 2 ch sp, ss to 1st t-ch at beg of round.

Round 2: 3 t-ch (counts as 1 tr), 2 ch back into 1 ch of previous round, * 1 dc in 3rd tr of next 5 tr shell, 5 tr in next dc, rep from * to last repeat, 1 dc in 3rd tr of next 5 tr shell, 2 tr in 1 ch at beg of round, ss to 3rd of 3 t-ch at beg of round.

Round 3: 1 t-ch (counts as dc), * 5 tr in next dc, 1 dc in 3rd tr of next 5 tr shell, rep from * to last repeat, 5 tr in next dc, ss to 1 t-ch at beg of round.

Rep round 2 once more. Fasten off.

Small flower

Using a 6 mm hook and dark pink yarn doubled, make a length of 4 ch, and join by working ss into the first of these ch.

Round 1: 1 t-ch (counts as 1 dc), * 3 ch, 1 dc, into ring rep from * four more times, 1 tr into 1 t-ch at beg of round (6 spaces).

Round 2: 1 t-ch (counts as 1 dc), 1 htr, 2 tr, 1 htr, 1 dc, all worked into first 1 tr sp, * 1 dc, 1 htr, 2 tr, 1 htr, 1 dc all worked into next 3 ch sp, rep from * four more times, ss to 1st 1 t-ch, fasten off.

Large flower

Using a 6 mm hook and working with pale pink yarn, held double, make a length of 4 ch, and join by working ss into the first of these ch.

Round 1: 3 t-ch (counts as 1 tr) 11 tr into ring, ss to 3rd of 3 t-ch at beg of round (12 tr).

Round 2: 1 t-ch (counts as 1 dc), skip 1st tr, * 4 ch, skip next 1 tr, 1 dc into next tr, rep from * four more times, 1 dtr into 1 t-ch at beg of round (6 spaces).

Round 3: 1 t-ch (counts as dc), (1 htr, 2 tr, 1 dtr, 2 tr, 1 htr, 1 dc), worked into first 1 tr sp,* 1 dc, 1 htr, 2 tr, 1 dtr, 2 tr, 1 htr, (1 dc, 1 htr, 2 tr, 1 dtr, 2 tr, 1 htr, 1 dc), worked into next 4 ch sp, rep from * four more times, ss to 1st 1 t-ch, fasten off.

Making up

Place the small flower onto the large flower and sew together. Sew a large button into the centre of the flower and a smaller button through the larger button. Attach the flower to the hat.

Weave in all ends.

Close-up of the flower.

ROUND GRANNY CUSHION

Brighten up a kitchen chair with this multicoloured granny cushion.

Size
41 cm (16 in) diameter

Materials
- 1 x 100 g ball each of King Cole Bamboo Cotton shades Saffron 637, Green 533, Cream 538

- (230 m/252 yd per ball)

- 1 x 4 mm crochet hook (USG/6)

- 4 x 18 mm buttons

- 1 x 41 cm (16 in) cushion pad

To substitute yarn:
Use any DK yarn that has a standard knit tension of 22 sts and 28/30 rows to 10 cm square worked on 4 mm (US6) needles.

Tension
Tension is not critical, but the diameter should measure 5.5 cm after two rounds, and 12 cm after six rounds. If your work is too small, change to a larger hook and start again; if it is too large, change to a smaller hook and start again.

Abbreviations
beg = beginning
bobble = yoh, insert hook into ring, yoh, hook back through ring (3 loops on hook), yoh and draw through 2 loops (2 loops left on hook). Then yoh and insert hook back into ring, yoh, hook back through ring (4 loops on hook), yoh and draw through 2 loops (3 loops left on hook), yoh and draw through all 3 loops
ch = chain
cluster = group of 3 tr

dc = double crochet
rep = repeat
shell = group of 7 tr
sp = space
ss = slip stitch
t-ch = turning chain
tr = treble
yoh = yarn over hook
2 tr bobble = yoh, insert hook into st, yoh, draw through, yoh draw through 2 loops, rep from * once more – working into the same st, yoh, draw through all 3 loops on the hook
3 tr bobble = yoh, insert hook into st, yoh, draw through, yoh, draw through 2 loops, rep from * twice more – working into the same st, yoh, draw through all 4 loops on the hook

Note:
Cut yarns as you go and weave in later.

The cushion makes a pretty accessory.

To make the cushion

Using a 4 mm hook and yellow yarn, make a length of 4 ch and join into a ring by working ss into the first of these ch.

Round 1: With yellow, 3 t-ch (counts as 1 tr), 1 tr into the ring, * 1 ch, work 1 bobble into the ring, rep from * 6 more times, work 1 dc into to 3rd of 3 t-ch at beg of round drawing the cream yarn through the last 2 loops of this stitch – do not turn work. (You will have 8 'bobbles', counting the first 2 tr as 1 bobble.)

Round 2: With cream, 3 t-ch (counts as 1 tr), 2 tr back into the space made by the last dc of previous round, * 1 ch, 3 tr into next 1 ch sp, rep from * 6 more times, 1 dc into 3rd of 3 t-ch at beg of round drawing the green yarn through the last 2 loops of this stitch – do not turn work. (You will have 8 x 3 tr clusters – work now measures 5.5 cm diameter.)

Round 3: With green, 1 t-ch (counts as dc), 1 dc back into the space made by the last dc of previous round, * 3 ch, 2 dc in next 1 ch sp, rep from * 6 more times, 1 tr worked into 1 t-ch at beg of round drawing the yellow yarn through the last 2 loops of this stitch – do not turn work. (You will have 8 x 3 ch spaces – counting the space made by the last tr as a 3 ch sp.)

Round 4: With yellow, 3 t-ch (counts as 1 tr), 3 tr back into the space made by the last tr of previous round, 1 tr into each of next 2 dc, * 4 tr into next 3 ch sp, 1 tr into each of next 2 dc, rep from * 6 more times, ss to 3rd of 3 t-ch at beg of round, drawing the cream yarn through the last 2 loops of this stitch – do not turn work (48 tr).

Round 5: With cream, 1 t-ch (counts as 1 dc), skip 1 tr at base of this ch, * 2 ch, skip 1 tr, 1 dc in next tr, rep from * to last 1 tr of

round, 1 tr into 1 t-ch at beg of round drawing the green yarn through the last 2 loops of this stitch – do not turn work. (You will have 24 x 2 ch spaces – counting the space made by the last tr as a 2 ch sp.)

Round 6: With green, 3 t-ch (counts as 1 tr), 2 tr back into the space made by the last tr of previous round, * 1 ch, 3 tr into next 2 ch sp, rep from * to last dc, end with 1 dc into to 3rd of 3 t ch at beg of round drawing the yellow yarn through the last 2 loops of this stitch – do not turn work. (You will have 24 x 3 tr clusters.)

Round 7: With yellow, 3 t-ch (counts as 1 tr), 2 tr back into the space made by the last dc of previous round, * 1 ch, 3 tr into next 1 ch sp, rep from * to last 3 tr cluster, end with 1 dc into to 3rd of 3 t ch at beg of round drawing the cream yarn through the last 2 loops of this stitch – do not turn work. (You will have 24 x 3 tr clusters.)

Round 8: With cream, work as for round 7, drawing green through last 2 loops.

Round 9: With green, 1 t-ch (counts as dc), 1 dc back into the space made by the last dc of previous round, * 3 ch, 2 dc in next 1 ch sp, rep from * to last 3 tr cluster end with 1 tr into 1 t-ch at beg of round drawing the yellow yarn through the last 2 loops of this stitch – do not turn work. (You will have 24 x 3 ch spaces counting the space made by the last tr as a 3 ch sp.)

Round 10: With yellow, 3 t-ch (counts as 1 tr), 2 tr back into the space made by the last tr of previous round, 1 tr into each of next 2 dc, * 3 tr into next 3 ch sp, 1 tr into each of next 2 dc, rep from * to end, ss to 3rd of 3 t-ch at beg of round, drawing the cream yarn through the last 2 loops of this stitch – do not turn work (120 tr).

Round 11: With cream, 1 t-ch (counts as 1 dc), skip 1 tr at base of this ch, * 2 ch, skip 2 tr, 1 dc in next tr, rep from * to last 2 tr of round, end with 1 tr into 1 t-ch at beg of round, drawing the green yarn through the last 2 loops of this stitch – do not turn work. (You will have 40 x 2 ch spaces – counting the space made by the last tr as a 2 ch sp.)

Round 12: With green, 3 t-ch (counts as 1 tr), 2 tr back into the space made by the last tr of previous round, * 1 ch, 3 tr into next 2 ch sp, rep from * to last ch, end with 1 dc into to 3rd of 3 t-ch at beg of round, drawing the yellow yarn through the last 2 loops of this stitch – do not turn work. (You will have 40 x 3 tr clusters.)

Round 13: With yellow, 3 t-ch (counts as 1 tr), 2 tr back into the space made by the last dc of previous round, * 1 ch, 3 tr into next 1 ch sp, rep from * to last 3 tr cluster, end with 1 dc into to 3rd of 3 t-ch at beg of round, drawing the cream yarn through the last 2 loops of this stitch – do not turn work. (You will have 40 x 3 tr clusters.)

Round 14: With cream, work as for round 13, pulling green through last 2 loops.

Round 15: With green, 1 t-ch (counts as dc), 1 dc back into the space made by the last dc of previous round, * 3 ch, 2 dc in next 1 ch sp, rep from * to last 3 tr cluster, end with 1 tr into 1 t-ch at beg of round, drawing the yellow yarn through the last 2 loops of this stitch – do not turn work. (You will have 40 x 3 ch spaces – counting the space made by the last tr as a 3 ch sp.)

Round 16: With yellow, 3 t-ch (counts as 1 tr), 2 tr back into the space made by the last tr of previous round, 1 tr into each of next 2 dc, * 3 tr into next 3 ch sp, 1 tr into each of next 2 dc, rep from * to end, ss to 3rd of 3 t-ch at beg of round, drawing the cream yarn through the last 2 loops of this stitch – do not turn work (200 tr).

Round 17: With cream, 1 t-ch (counts as 1 dc), skip 1 tr at base of this ch, * 3 ch, skip 3 tr, 1 dc in next tr, rep from * to last 3 tr of round, end with 1 tr into 1 t-ch at beg of round, drawing the green yarn through the last 2 loops of this stitch – do not turn work. (You will have 50 x 3 ch spaces – counting the space made by the last tr as a 3 ch sp.)

Round 18: With green, 3 t-ch (counts as 1 tr), 2 tr back into the space made by the last tr of previous round, * 1 ch, 3 tr into next 2 ch sp, rep from * to last dc, end with 1 dc into 3rd of 3 t-ch at beg of round, drawing the yellow yarn through the last 2 loops of this stitch – do not turn work. (You will have 50 x 3 tr clusters.)

Round 19: With yellow, 3 t-ch (counts as 1 tr), 2 tr back into the space made by the last dc of previous round, * 1 ch, 3 tr into next 1 ch sp, rep from * to last 3 tr cluster, end with 1 dc into to 3rd of 3 t-ch at beg of round, drawing the cream yarn through the last 2 loops of this stitch – do not turn work. (You will have 50 x 3 tr clusters.)

Round 20: With cream, work as for round 19, drawing green through last 2 loops.

Round 21: With green, 1 t-ch (counts as dc), * 4 ch, 1 dc in next 1 ch sp, rep from * ending 3 ch and ss to 1 t-ch at beg of round. (You will have 50 x 3 ch spaces.)

Fasten off.
Weave in all ends.
Work second side to match.

Use bright buttons to make this cushion even more cheerful.

Border

Place the two cushion pieces WS together and match up the pattern at the outer edge. With a 4 mm hook and yellow yarn, insert hook through any dc of last row, inserting the hook through the dc of both layers. Work as below.

Joining round:

yoh, draw through the two dc, yoh and draw through the 1 loop on hook, * work 7 tr under both of the next pair of 4 ch sp, work 1 dc through next pair of dc, rep from * 40 more times (41 shells), then work as before **but** working though front layer of work only, eight more times, finish with 7 tr in last single 4 ch sp, ss to 1st ch of round.

Fasten off and weave in all ends. This leaves an opening of 9 x 4 ch spaces to insert cushion pad. Sew buttons to correspond with every alternate 4 ch sp, so that they act as button loops.

LACE COLLAR

Dress up a plain neckline with a simple tied collar.

Size
124[130] cm (48¾[51] in) wide
including ties

Materials
- 1 x 50 g balls of Debbie Bliss
  Luxury Silk DK shade 007 Duck
  Egg (100 m/110 yd per 50 g ball)

- 1 x 4 mm crochet hook (USG/6)

To substitute yarn:
Use correct length of any DK yarn
that has a standard knit tension of
22 sts and 28/30 rows to 10 cm
square worked on 4 mm (US6)
needles.

Tension
The tension is 14 tr and 10 rows
= 10 cm (4 in). When you have
worked the first two rows the
work should measure 124[130] cm
(48¾[51] in) wide. In order for the
collar to be the size given, you will
need to achieve this measurement.
If your work is too small, change to
a larger hook and start again; if it is
too large, change to a smaller hook
and start again.

Abbreviations
beg = beginning
ch = chain
dc = double crochet
prev = previous
rem = remaining
rep = repeat
sp = space
ss = slip stitch
t-ch = turning chain
tr = treble

This pretty collar dresses up a plain neckline.

Make the collar

Using a 4 mm hook, make a length of 155[163] ch and work as follows:

Row 1:   1 tr in 4th ch from hook, 1 tr in each ch to end (153[161] tr – counting 1st 3 ch as 1 tr).

Row 2:   3 t-ch (counts as 1st tr), 1 tr in each of next 48 tr, place coloured thread as marker in this last st, 1 tr in next tr, * 2 tr in next tr, 1 tr in each of next 3 tr, rep from * 13[15] times in all, 2 tr in next tr, 1 tr in each of next 2 tr and place coloured thread as marker in this last st, 1 tr in each of rem 48 tr – working last tr in 3rd of 3 t-ch at beg of prev row. Fasten off and cut yarn.

Row 3:   Turn work and using a 4 mm hook, rejoin yarn with ss to 1st marker (the last marker placed). Now work as follows: 3 ch (counts as 1 dc and 2 ch), skip this marked tr and next tr, * 1 dc in next tr, skip 2 tr, 7 tr in next tr, skip 2 tr, 1 dc in next tr, 5 ch, skip next 3 tr, rep from * 5[6] more times, 1 dc in next tr, skip 2 tr, 7 tr in next tr, skip next 2 tr, 1 dc in next tr, skip 1 tr, 2 ch, 1 dc in marked tr. Turn.

Row 4:   1 t-ch (counts as 1 dc), * 1 ch, (1 dtr in next tr, 1 ch) x 7, 1 dc in next 5 ch sp, rep from * 6[7] more times, working the last dc in 1st of 3 ch at beg of prev row.

Row 5:   1 ch (counts as 1 dc), * 3 ch, 1 dc in next 1 ch sp, rep from to end working last dc in the 1 t-ch.

Fasten off and sew in all ends.

Close-up of the collar.

ABBREVIATIONS

Standard abbreviations used throughout this book are given below. More specific abbreviations are given with each pattern.

beg = beginning

ch = chain

cm = centimetre(s)

cont = continue

dc = double crochet

DK = double knitting

dtr = double treble

htr = half treble

in = inch(es)

MC = main colour

mm = millimetre(s)

prev = previous

rem = remaining

rep = repeat

RS = right side

sp = space

ss = slip stitch

st(s) = stitch(es)

t-ch = turning chain

tr = treble

ttr = triple treble

WS = wrong side

yd = yard

yoh = yarn over hook

htr 2 tog = * yoh, insert hook into st, yoh, draw through, * yoh, draw through two loops, working into next st, rep from * to * once, yoh, draw through all four loops on the hook. These 2 sts now count as 1 st.

* shows the beginning of a pattern sequence – different numbers of asterisks refer to different sections of work

() contains a pattern sequence or information such as the stitch count

[] contains instructions (usually numbers) for different sizes

STOCKISTS

Artesano
For a list of stockists visit the website at:
www.artesanoyarns.co.uk or phone 01189 503350.

Brittany Hooks
Brittany hooks and needles are also available
from Artesano.

Colinette
Colinette yarns can be bought direct from their
website, where you will also find a list of stockists:
www.colinette.com or phone 01938 810128.

Debbie Bliss
A list of stockists can be found at
www.designeryarns.uk.com or phone 01535 664222.

DMC
For a list of stockists visit the website at:
www.dmccreative.co.uk or phone 01162 754000.

Hayfield
Available through Sirdar. For a list of stockists see
the Sirdar website.

James C Brett
For your nearest stockist contact James C. Brett
through their website www.jameschrett.co.uk or
phone 01274 565959 / 01274 569381.

King Cole
For your nearest stockist contact King Cole
through their website www.kingcole.co.uk
or phone 01535 650230.

Noro
A list of stockists can be found at
www.designeryarns.uk.com or phone 01535 664222.

Patons
A list of stockists can be found at
www.coatscrafts.co.uk or phone 01484 681881.

Rico
See more of the Rico yarns at www.rico-design.de
and don't forget to click on the Union Jack for the
English version. For your nearest Rico stockist email
info@rico-design.de or phone 49(0) 5272602-0.

Rowan
A list of stockists can be found at
www.coatscrafts.co.uk or phone 01484 681881.

Sirdar
A list of stockists can be found at www.sirdar.co.uk
or phone 01924 231682.

ACKNOWLEDGEMENTS

I would like to say a huge thank you to all those who
have been involved in the creation of this book.
Especially to my photographer Jess Withers for all her
lovely photos and to the models Karen, Izzy, Judah and
Nathan, who made the photography so interesting.
Also to my husband, Mark, who made meals, held yarn
while I wound it into balls, made pompoms, and also
modelled for me. Many of the photos were taken in the
oh-so-beautiful garden of friends Angie and Mike, so a
big thank you to them too.

My crocheters, Dorothy, Sheila, and Zoe, were
of course absolutely vital as they checked the
patterns and made many of the items for the
photographs. I'm very grateful to the companies
who supplied the yarns – they are listed above.

And finally, my thanks to Bloomsbury Publishing and
especially to my editor, Agnes Upshall, who gave me
the opportunity to write this book.

INDEX